Test Expert

Writing Practice for **CELPIP**®

Christien Lee

Thanks to M and K (and T as well) for putting up with me while I wrote this. I love you all.

TABLE OF CONTENTS

HOW TO USE THIS BOOK

This book is designed to help you improve your ability to write effective, high-scoring responses to Writing Task 1 and Writing Task 2 in the CELPIP Test. It is not designed to be a complete guide to writing in English. Instead, it offers advice that is specific to the tasks you will see in the writing section of the CELPIP-G test. If you study this guide carefully and practice writing responses based on the expert responses in this guide, you will become a more effective writer.

Key Features

This book has numerous features designed to help you write more effective responses to the questions you will see in the CELPIP Test:

- Detailed introductions to the CELPIP Test as well as Writing Task 1 and Writing Task 2.

- Step-by-step guides for how to write effective responses to Task 1 and Task 2.

- Forty-two writing topics; 21 for Writing Task 1 and an additional 21 for Writing Task 2.

- Forty-two model responses written by a test expert, many with detailed analysis and advice.

- Ten writing practice exercises to help you avoid common mistakes and write natural sentences.

- Ten writing challenges to give you practice responding to typical writing topics in CELPIP.

- Lists of over 120 useful words and phrases that you can copy and use in your own responses.

- Several valuable tips to help you study in the most effective way to improve your score.

Suggested Approach

You can use this book in any way that will benefit you, but following these ten steps is recommended:

STEP 1   Read the introduction to CELPIP that starts on page 7. Then read the introduction to Writing Task 1 that starts on page 11.

STEP 2   Study the analysis of a response to writing task that starts on page 13.

STEP 3   Read the step-by-step guide to Writing Task 1 that starts on page 15.

STEP 4   Look at Topic 1 for Writing Task 1 on page 18. Read the analysis of the topic and the expert's response.

STEP 5   Type out the Expert's Response to Topic 1. This step is optional, but it will help you learn and use the expert's perfect vocabulary, grammar, and organization. You will probably get even more benefit if you type out the response several times.

STEP 6   Complete the Writing Practice on page 20. Then turn to page 21 and study the list of useful phrases before completing the Writing Challenge under test conditions.

STEP 7   Repeat steps 4 to 6 for Writing Topics 2, 3, 4, and 5.

STEP 8   Repeat steps 2 to 7 for Writing Task 2.

STEP 9   Look at the additional writing topics starting on page 38 for Task 1 and on page 68 for Task 2. Write a response to at least one of these topics under test conditions every day. Then compare your response with the sample response at the back of this book.

STEP 10   After you have finished all of the writing challenges and practice tasks in this book, find other writing topics and continue practicing every day until the day of your CELPIP Test. (You will find suggestions for finding additional topics or coming up with your own topics on pages 40 and 71.)

Note that when you complete a Writing Challenge in Step 6 or write a response to an additional topic in Step 9, you may find it helpful to follow this procedure:

- While writing, work under test conditions. This means finishing your response in 27 minutes (for Task 1) or 26 minutes (for Task 2), typing your response rather than writing it by hand, and not using a dictionary or other reference book.

- After writing, ask a teacher (or somebody else whose judgement you trust) to review your response and provide some feedback. Then review your response yourself and find at least five things to improve.

About the Author

The author, Christien Lee, was born in the UK, but has lived in Canada since 2002. He started teaching in 1992, and has specialized in helping people pass English language tests since 1997. These tests include CELPIP, IELTS, TOEFL, TOEIC, MELAB, PTE Academic, and Cambridge tests like FCE and CAE.

In addition to his work as a language teacher, he has been a teacher-trainer, a curriculum developer, a materials writer, a language training consultant, an e-learning developer, a programmer, and an author.

He has written the following books:

- A TOEFL textbook published by Oxford University Press

- A MELAB study guide published by Cambridge Michigan Language Assessments

- An LPI Writing guide published by Paragon Testing Enterprises
  (this is the organization that develops and administers the CELPIP Test)

- An academic skills book based on TED Talks published by Cengage / National Geographic Learning

Speaking Guide

The author of this writing guide is currently working on a similar book that provides practice for the speaking section of the CELPIP Test. This book, which will be available soon, will include a detailed introduction to each speaking task, model responses for each task, practice and challenge activities, and a list of useful words and phrases.

(Note that the image shown is not the final design.)

INTRODUCTION to CELPIP®

CELPIP is a computer-based English language proficiency test. The name stands for Canadian English Language Proficiency Index Program. There are three versions of the test: CELPIP-General (or CELPIP-G), which tests reading, listening, speaking, and writing; CELPIP-LS, which tests listening and speaking only; and CELPIP-Academic. **This book is designed to help people taking CELPIP-G only. If you are taking CELPIP-LS, this book will not benefit you.**

The Department of Citizenship and Immigration (CIC) Canada has designated CELPIP-G as an accredited test to demonstrate proficiency in English. It is typically taken by people in order to become a permanent resident of Canada or in order to prove their skills for immigration to Canada under a program such as the Federal Skilled Worker Program or Federal Skilled Trades Program. In total, CELPIP-G takes around three hours to complete.

There are four sections in CELPIP-G:

	Section	Description	Time
1	Listening	The listening section has six scored parts and one unscored part. You will listen to two conversations between two people, listen to one person interviewing another person, watch a video that shows two or three people talking, and listen to two talks or reports.	~40 minutes
2	Reading	The reading section has four scored parts and one unscored part. You will read several letters, emails, and short texts. You will also have to read information about diagrams or photographs.	60 minutes
3	Writing	The writing section has two scored tasks. It does not have any unscored tasks. You will write one email based on information that is given to you. You will also write a response to a survey question.	53 minutes
4	Speaking	The speaking section has eight scored tasks and one unscored practice task. The tasks include expressing your opinion about a topic, giving advice to somebody, describing a personal experience, and describing what you can see in a picture.	~20 minutes

CELPIP-G is a computerized test. Every part of the test will take place on a computer, including speaking and writing. If you are not comfortable using a computer, practice as much as possible before your test.

Introduction to the Writing Test

Writing is the third part of CELPIP-G. At the start of the writing test, you will see specific instructions about how to answer the writing test. The instructions will look similar to this:

CELPIP-General - Writing Test

ⓘ Writing Test Instructions

- There are 2 tasks in this test.

- Use the computer keyboard to write your response.

- You can see how many words you have written by looking at the bottom of the writing area to see the word count.

- You have 27 minutes to complete Task 1 and 26 minutes to complete Task 2. Watch the timer in the top right corner to make sure that you complete each task before the time is up.

- If you do not finish Task 1 in 27 minutes, the screen will move to Task 2. You cannot go back.

- You have 53 minutes to complete the Writing Test.

When you take the writing test, you must type your answers. **You cannot write your answers by hand.** As you are typing, you will have access to features such as word count, spell check, and basic editing functions like cut, copy, paste, delete, undo, and redo.

The writing section lasts approximately 53 minutes and has two scored tasks. These tasks are intended to be similar to the kinds of writing in English you might have to do in everyday life:

Task	Question Type	Required Words	Time
1	Writing an email	150-200	27 minutes
2	Responding to survey questions	150-200	26 minutes

How the Writing Test is Scored

In total, four different specially-trained raters will assess your responses: two raters will assess your response to Writing Task 1, and two different raters will assess your response to Writing Task 2.

Each rater will assess your response according to four criteria:

Explanation of Scoring Criteria

1 Coherence / Meaning
How clear your ideas are and how well your ideas work together

- Have you explained your ideas clearly?

- Have you organized your response in a way that makes it easy for the rater to follow your ideas?

- Have you shown the ability to express information precisely and with deep meaning?

2 Lexical Range
How accurately and naturally you use vocabulary

- Does your response have a sufficient range of vocabulary to complete the task well?

- Have you shown the ability to use natural words and phrases to express ideas accurately?

3 Readability / Comprehensibility
How fluent your writing is and how easy it is to understand

- Are grammar, spelling, punctuation, or word errors likely to confuse the reader?

- Have you used a variety of different sentence types, including simple, compound, and complex?

- Does your response have clear, well-organized, logical paragraphs and appropriate formatting?

- Have you used connectors and transition words and phrases clearly and effectively?

4 Task Fulfillment
How well your response addresses the task

- Does your response answer every part of the task effectively?

- Is your response long enough?

- Is the tone of your response appropriate, or is it too formal or informal?

The rater will assign you a score out of 12 for each criterion. Your final mark from each rater will be the average of the scores for each criterion. Your final score for the writing test will be the average of the four scores you received from the raters.

STUDY TIPS FOR CELPIP®

These study tips will help you achieve a good score in the writing section of CELPIP.

Study Tip 1 – Get Authentic Practice

When you type your own responses to CELPIP topics, you can get authentic practice by using the free CELPIP sample test available from Paragon Testing Enterprises. Follow these steps:

- Visit `https://secure.paragontesting.ca/InstructionalProducts/` and click on the orange button marked "Start Sample Test."
- Choose "Free Online Sample Test - G" from the drop-down menu and then click "OK."
- Click the orange button marked "Start" and then choose "Writing" from the drop-down menu.
- Click "Next" when the writing directions appear. You will see the screen for Writing Task 1 and the timer will start counting down. To practice Writing Task 2, click "Next" again.
- In the space, type your response to a topic from this book rather than the official topic on the screen.

  (Note that when you use this free sample test, your response will not be saved. To save it, copy and paste your finished response into a document on your computer and click save.)

Study Tip 2 – Be Accurate and Natural Rather Than Advanced

The scoring criteria for CELPIP do NOT say your writing must be advanced. To score well, it is often better to use a variety of relatively simple English that is accurate and natural rather than trying to use advanced language, but using it in incorrect or unnatural ways. This is especially true because advanced language that has mistakes is more likely to confuse the rater, and this can have a significant effect on your overall score.

Study Tip 3 – Write about Familiar Topics

When deciding which ideas to write about, always try to write about something familiar that you have previously written (or spoken) about in English. Writing about an unfamiliar topic will probably cause you to take more time writing your response, so you may not finish. You will also probably make more mistakes.

Study Tip 4 – Read Like a Writer

When you read something in English, think like a writer. Notice how the writer uses words and phrases to express his or her meaning. Also notice how the writer uses grammar and punctuation. Then memorize some of the best words, phrases, and grammar structures and use them in your own writing.

TASK 1: INTRODUCTION

When you begin the writing test, you will see Task 1. The computer screen will look something like this:

Writing Task 1: Writing an Email	Time remaining: 26 minutes 43 seconds
ⓘ Read the following information. You went out for dinner at a restaurant with your family yesterday last month. When you checked your credit card statement today, you saw that you had been charged twice for the meal.	**ⓘ In about 150-200 words, write an email to the restaurant manager. Your email should do the following things:** • Say when and why you went to the restaurant. • Describe the problem in detail. • Explain how the manager should fix the issue.

At the top of the screen, you will see the title bar, which explains which writing task you are currently responding to, and how much time you have left. For Task 1, you have 27 minutes in total. When the time is up, the computer will automatically proceed to Writing Task 2.

Writing Task 1: Writing an Email	Time remaining: 26 minutes 43 seconds

ⓘ Read the following information.

You went out for dinner at a restaurant with your family yesterday last month. When you checked your credit card statement today, you saw that you had been charged twice for the meal.

On the left side of the screen, you will see some background information that describes a situation. You will need to read this information in order to understand the task.

On the right of the screen, you will see the prompt. This explains who you should write to. This information will help you decide how to begin your email. For example, if the prompt tells you to write to the manager of a restaurant, you might begin "Dear Sir or Madam" or perhaps "Dear Manager." In contrast, if the prompt tells you to write to a sister or another family member, you might begin "Hi," "Hi Mary," or "Dear Sis."

> ⓘ **In about 150-200 words, write an email to the restaurant manager. Your email should do the following things:**
>
> - Say when and why you went to the restaurant.
> - Describe the problem in detail.
> - Explain how the manager should fix the issue.

The prompt also mentions what information your email should include. Typically, the prompt includes three things that your email should do. These are in the form of bullet points, and usually begin with imperative verbs like "say," "describe," or "explain." In order to get a good score, your response *must* include sentences that cover all this information. As a result, it is very important that you read the information carefully and understand it fully.

The white box below the prompt is where you should type your response. As you type, a scroll bar will appear so that you can see your whole response. You will see the word count below the white box.

As a general rule, a good response to Writing Task 1 will include five elements:

- A greeting, such as "Dear Sir or Madam," or "Hi Mary." The greeting should be short.

- A first body paragraph. This paragraph will often explain why you are writing. In general, the paragraph should also cover the information in the first bullet point in the prompt.

- A second body paragraph. Generally, speaking, this paragraph should cover the information in the second bullet point in the prompt.

- A third body paragraph. Generally, speaking, this paragraph should cover the information in the third bullet point in the prompt.

- A closing, such as "I look forward to hearing from you," "Please contact me if you need more information," or simply "Thanks." You may also wish to add a name below the closing. This does not have to be your real name.

Because Task 1 questions follow a standard pattern, it is likely that you can use these elements in every response.

TASK 1: ANALYSIS OF A RESPONSE

Read the prompt and response by a test expert on this page. Then read the analysis of the response on the next page. This will help you understand how to write effective, high-scoring responses to Task 1 prompts.

Writing Task 1: Writing an Email | Time remaining: 00 minutes 43 seconds

 Read the following information.

You went out for dinner at a restaurant with your family yesterday last month. When you checked your credit card statement today, you saw that you had been charged twice for the meal.

 In about 150-200 words, write an email to the restaurant manager. Your email should do the following things:

- Say when and why you went to the restaurant.
- Describe the problem in detail.
- Explain how the manager should fix the issue.

> To Whom It May Concern
>
> My family and I visited your restaurant last month. It was my wife's birthday, and we wanted to have a delicious family meal as a celebration. The food and service were both good, but unfortunately you charged too much. This is why I am writing to you.
>
> I ordered the salmon salad, my wife had pasta with chicken, and our children both had pizza and salad. We only ordered water. According to your website, the total cost of this meal should have been $72. Unfortunately, when I checked my credit card statement today, I saw that we were charged for this meal twice.
>
> Please could you email me today to let me know when you can refund this second charge to my credit card? If you prefer, you can telephone me at my office on 123 456 7890 (extension 321).
>
> I look forward to hearing from you soon.
>
> Mr R Smith

To Whom It May Concern

My family and I visited your restaurant last month. It was my wife's birthday, and we wanted to have a delicious family meal as a celebration. The food and service were both good, but unfortunately you charged too much. This is why I am writing to you.

I ordered the salmon salad, my wife had pasta with chicken, and our children both had pizza and salad. We only ordered water. According to your website, the total cost of this meal should have been $72. Unfortunately, when I checked my credit card statement today, I saw that we were charged for this meal twice.

Please could you email me today to let me know when you can refund this second charge to my credit card? If you prefer, you can telephone me at my office on 123 456 7890 (extension 321).

I look forward to hearing from you soon.

Mr R Smith

Every email should begin with a greeting. "To Whom It May Concern" is a good greeting for formal emails when you do not know the name of the other person.

The opening paragraph should explain why you are writing the email. It should also address the task given in the first bullet in the prompt. The writer does both of these things well.

The second paragraph should address the task in the second bullet in the prompt. The writer does this very well, with plenty of specific, believable details.

The third paragraph should address the task in the third bullet in the prompt. Again, the writer does this effectively and includes specific, believable details.

It is often a good idea to add a closing line to each email. Because the writer wants the manager to contact him, "I look forward to hearing from you soon" sounds very natural.

Finish your email with a name. As a general rule, it is better not to use your own name. If you use an imaginary name, choose one that is easy to spell.

This email, which has 156 words, is clearly organized, well written, and addresses the task fully. Its only weakness is that the language is deliberately somewhat simple in places. **It would probably score 11 – 12.**

TASK 1: STEP-BY-STEP GUIDE

Writing Task 1 questions follow a standard pattern. As a result, you can follow the same steps each time you write a Task 1 response either for practice or during the official CELPIP test.

Step 1

Read the background information carefully. Look for useful information that will help you understand your task. For example, does the background information mention a negative experience that you will need to complain about, or does it describe a situation in which you will need to ask somebody for help?

Also make a note of any information that will help you respond to the prompt. For instance, if the situation asks you to complain, look for specific details that explain why you are complaining.

Next read the prompt carefully. Notice who you should write to and what information your message should include. This information will be explained in the three bullet points. Decide how best to organize your response. In most cases, the best organization will be the five-element organization explained on page 12:

- A greeting
- A paragraph that says why you are writing and addresses the first bullet point of the prompt
- A paragraph that addresses the second bullet point of the prompt
- A paragraph that addresses the third bullet point of the prompt
- A closing sentence or phrase, and then a name

In some cases, however, you may think that two of the paragraphs should be combined. For instance, you might feel it would be more natural if you write one paragraph that addresses both the first and second bullet points, or one that addresses the second and third bullets. (Note that unless you are completely confident that doing this will make your response easier for the rater to understand, you should probably stick with the five-element organization.)

Plan to spend up to two minutes on Step 1, but doing it in less time is better, if possible.

Step 2

After reading the background information and prompt carefully, and after deciding how to organize your response, you should brainstorm ideas. This means to think of ideas that match the task, and to decide which of those ideas you will include in your response.

When you brainstorm, you should:

- Think of ideas, details, and examples that match either the background information or the things mentioned in the prompt that you need to address

(You can also brainstorm words, phrases, and grammar structures that would be natural to use when you type your response to the prompt.)

If you wish, you can make a note of your ideas on a piece of paper. This is not necessary, but it will help you remember your ideas when you are typing your response, so it is usually a good idea to do this.

For example, for the Task 1 topic shown on page 18, you might brainstorm and note down ideas like these:

> - problem
>   = workmen start 6AM, finish 10PM
>   = loud noise from equipm & shouting
> - where live = across street from site
> - affects life
>   = cannot sleep well
>   = work at home so cannot concentrate
> - want = workers should work usual hours (9 to 5)

After you have brainstormed your ideas, decide which of them you will include in your response. If you came up with many ideas, you will probably not have enough time to include all of them, so just include the ones that are most familiar to you. These will be easier for you to write about than less familiar ideas, so you will probably be able to write about them more quickly and with fewer mistakes.

Plan to spend up to five minutes on Step 2. This may seem like a long time, but responses that are written without any brainstorming or plan are often more disorganized and have more mistakes.

Step 3

After brainstorming your ideas, you need to type your response. Remember: you will not be able to write your response by hand.

When you type, you should follow the organization you decided on in Step 1 and write about the ideas you chose in Step 2. This is where having notes can be very helpful.

As you type each sentence, focus on the following things:

- Be careful about mistakes, especially basic mistakes like forgetting to put -s or -ed on the ends of words, or using the wrong tense. Mistakes like these are likely to reduce your score.

- Avoid writing sentences that are too long because these are likely to confuse the rater, which may affect your score. As a rule, sentences up to 20 words long are generally OK.

- Make sure each sentence directly addresses one of the points from the prompt (or adds a relevant detail or example). If your sentences are off-topic, your score might be affected.

- Do not use too many simple sentences – good responses usually have a balance of simple, compound, and complex sentences. (If you are not sure what these terms mean, check a grammar book or look up the information online.)

Spend as much time as you need on Step 3. Do NOT try to save time at the end; it is better to write a full response than to write a shorter one just so you have a few minutes left at the end.

Step 4

Even if you finish Task 1 early, you cannot add any remaining minutes or seconds to the time you have for Task 2. As a result, if you have any time left at the end, try to improve your response:

- Check you have used clear **connectors** (e.g., *As a result*) and **sequence words** (e.g., *Firstly*).

- Look for opportunities to add details or examples to make your ideas and points clearer.

- Fix any mistakes that you notice. (But keep in mind that you will probably not be able to fix all of your mistakes; as a result, fixing mistakes is unlikely to affect your overall score.)

TASK 1: TOPIC 1.1

Topic

Read this Writing Task 1 topic. What information in the topic is important?
How could this information help you to write an effective response to the topic?

Writing Task 1: Writing an Email	27 minutes
 **Read the following information.** You live in an apartment near a building site. Recently, the construction workers have begun working on the site from early every morning and continuing until late in the evening. Their work disturbs you because it makes a lot of noise.	**In about 150-200 words, write an email to the owner of the building company. Your email should do the following things:** • Give information about where you live. • Describe the problem and how it affects you. • Say how you think the owner could resolve the issue.

Analysis

Read this analysis of the topic by a test expert. Do the expert's ideas about the topic match your ideas?

The background information describes a negative situation. Specifically, it explains that you are being disturbed by noise from a construction site. From this, you can understand that you will need to write a complaint email. This is a common type of email writing task in CELPIP.

The prompt tells you to write to a company owner, which means your email should be relatively formal. It also tells you to do three things. First, you have to give information about where you live. A good response will make it clear that your home is close to the building site.

Second, you have to describe the problem and say how it affects you. A good response will paraphrase the background information from the topic. Copying too many words and phrases may have an effect on your score. In addition, a good response will give specific details or examples about how the noise affects you. Just saying "The noise disturbs me" or "There is too much noise" is not specific or detailed enough.

Finally, you have to say how you think the owner could resolve the issue. A good response will include one or more specific and detailed suggestions to improve the situation.

Expert's Response

Read this response by a test expert and the detailed analysis that explains why it is a good response.

Dear Company Owner

I live at 123 New Street in Newtown, Manitoba. My home is just across the street from the construction site operated by your company at 128 New Street.

I am writing to complain about noise from the construction site. Since last month, people have been working on the site from approximately 6AM to 10PM each day. The workers often shout and use noisy equipment. This has a big impact on my life. For one thing, the noise disturbs my sleep. For another thing, I work from home, but the noise makes it difficult for me to concentrate.

I would like you to instruct your workers to keep regular business hours. This means that they should start work no earlier than 9AM each day, and finish no later than 5PM each day. This would not be perfect for me, as I would still find it hard to focus when working at home, but it would certainly improve the situation. I am sure that other people living on my street would feel happier if your workers adopted this schedule.

Thank you

Mr R Smith

The greeting is relatively formal. An alternative would be "Dear Sir or Madam".

In the first paragraph, the writer clearly covers the first bullet point in the prompt. The address that the writer uses is obviously fake. In general, it is better not to use your real name or address.

In the second paragraph, the writer clearly covers the second bullet point in the prompt. Notice how the writer adds specific, believable details such as the time when the work begins and ends, and the causes of the noise. The writer also gives two examples of how the problem affects him, which is good.

In the third paragraph, the writer clearly covers the third bullet point in the prompt. Again, the writer adds specific details about times. In the final sentence, the writer explains how other people would also benefit from his suggestion, which is a natural, believable thing to say.

The writer closes the email by saying "thank you." Because the writer has asked the other person to do something, this is a natural way to end.

The writer uses a fake name to end the email. Because he does not know the name of the person he is writing to, he uses only his initial "R" rather than his first name.

185 words

This response has excellent coherence and meaning, good lexical range, very good readability and comprehensibility, and great task fulfillment. **Like all responses in this book, it would likely score 11 – 12.**

Practice Topic 1.1

Many test-takers make mistakes with prepositions (words like in, on, or with). Such errors may reduce a response's overall score. Type out this response to a practice topic. As you type, add in the correct preposition at each of the ten blanks. When you have finished, check your answers on page 72.

Writing Task 1: Writing an Email	27 minutes

ℹ **Read the following information.** You live near a park. Recently, some students from a local college have been spending time in the park in the evenings and at night. They talk loudly, play noisy games, and listen to loud music.	ℹ **In about 150-200 words, write an email to the city council. Your email should do the following things:** • Give information about where you live. • Describe the problem and how it affects you. • Say what you would like the city council to do about the problem.

Dear Sir or Madam

I live [1_____] 123 New Street in Newtown, Manitoba. My home is just across the street from the entrance [2_____] North Lake Park.

I am writing to complain about noise [3_____] the park. Since last month, some students from Newtown College have been hanging out in the park from approximately 8PM [4_____] late at night. They do this most days, but especially [5_____] weekends. The students talk and play music loudly, and sometimes they even play soccer or other sports and games. This has a big impact on my life because the noise makes it hard [6_____] me and my family to sleep.

I would like you to put up signs in North Lake Park asking people to be quiet if they use the park in the evening or [7_____] night. Alternatively, I would like you to lock the park [8_____] 8PM so that nobody can hang out there after dark and disturb others [9_____] being noisy. I am sure that other people living on my street would feel happier if you adopted one [10_____] these suggestions.

Thank you

Mr R Smith

Useful Language

These words and phrases may help you write an effective response to a Task 1 writing topic, especially one similar to the topics on this page and pages 18 and 20. There are more useful phrases on page 102.

For one thing, ...	*Use this phrase to introduce one point or reason for your opinion*
For another thing, ...	*Use this phrase to introduce a second point or reason for your opinion*
I am sure that other people ...	*Use this phrase when you want to introduce an opinion that other people are likely to share*
I am writing to complain about ...	*Use this phrase to introduce something you wish to complain about*
I would like you to ...	*Use this phrase when you want another person to perform a particular task or take a specific action*
This means that ...	*Use these words either to clarify the meaning of an idea you have just mentioned, or to talk about the result of something*

Challenge Topic 1.1

Type a response to this Writing Task 1 challenge topic in 27 minutes. Use the expert's response on page 19 as a guide. (See page 10 for a suggestion about how to get authentic practice when you type your response.) When you have finished, compare your response to the suggested response on page 72.

Writing Task 1: Writing an Email	27 minutes
❶ **Read the following information.** A popular new nightclub has opened near where you live. The noise from the nightclub is very loud, and many people who visit the club are also noisy when they arrive and leave.	❶ **In about 150-200 words, write an email to the owner of the nightclub. Your email should do the following things:** • Give information about where you live. • Describe the problem and say how it affects you. • Say how you think the owner could resolve the issue.

TASK 1: TOPIC 1.2

Topic

Read this Writing Task 1 topic. What information in the topic is important?
How could this information help you to write an effective response to the topic?

Writing Task 1: Writing an Email	27 minutes
ⓘ Read the following information. You are a professor at a university. One of your students has excellent ideas and studies hard. However, this person is thinking about dropping out of university and finding a job.	**ⓘ In about 150-200 words, write an email to your student. Your email should do the following things:** • Explain why you think this person is a good student. • Describe some of the disadvantages of dropping out. • Mention some benefits of graduating from university.

Analysis

Read this analysis of the topic by a test expert. Do the expert's ideas about the topic match your ideas?

The background information says that you are a university professor. From this, you can imagine that your email should be relatively formal. Specifically, the background information describes a situation that requires you to give advice to someone. This is a common type of email writing task in CELPIP.

The prompt tells you to write to your student. This tells you that it would be natural to use the student's first name (e.g., "Mary") rather than his or her family name (e.g., "Ms Jones"). The prompt also tells you to do three things. First, you have to give information about why you think this person is a good student. A good response will give one or more details or examples that explain this clearly.

Second, you have to discuss some disadvantages of dropping out of university. Because the prompt says "some of the disadvantages," a good response must mention at least two disadvantages.

Finally, you have to mention some benefits of graduating from university. Again, the prompt says "some benefits," so a good response will need to discuss at least two specific (not general) benefits.

Expert's Response

Read this response by a test expert and the detailed analysis that explains why it is a good response.

Dear Mary

I have heard that you are considering dropping out of university. I have been impressed with your ideas and with how hard you study. In my view you are a good student, and it is my hope that you will reconsider your plan.

I see two problems with dropping out. First, employers will see from your resume that you quit university. This might make them feel you are somebody who quits easily, which could make them decide not to hire you. And second, the economy is not doing well at the moment and few companies are hiring workers. In my opinion, now is not a good time to look for work.

These days, most employers want to hire those who have a university education, so graduating will make it easier for you to find employment. In addition, in a few years, the economy might be doing better, and more companies may be willing to hire people. For these two reasons, I strongly advise you to continue your studies.

Please come to my office anytime if you wish to discuss this further.

Professor Smith

The prompt says the professor is writing to a student he or she knows. For this reason, it is natural to use the student's first name here.

In the first paragraph, the writer explains why he or she thinks the student is a good student. This clearly addresses the first bullet in the prompt.

In the second paragraph, the writer covers the second bullet in the prompt. The first sentence of the paragraph states that the writer will mention two disadvantages. Then the writer introduces each disadvantage with a clear signpost expression: "First, …" and "And second, …"

In the third paragraph, the writer clearly covers the third bullet in the prompt by discussing two benefits of graduating from university. In this case, the writer does not use a signpost expression before the first benefit, but does before the second benefit ("In addition, …"). In the final sentence, the writer explicitly advises the student to continue studying. The prompt does not say that the writer needs to do this, but it is a natural thing to include in an email like this.

The writer closes the email by offering to give further support if needed. This is a natural way to close an email like this one.

As usual, the writer uses a common, easy-to-spell fake name.

This response has 185 words, excellent coherence and meaning, good lexical range, high readability and comprehensibility, and great task fulfillment. **Like all responses in this book, it would likely score 11 – 12.**

Practice Topic 1.2

Many test-takers make mistakes with tenses, such as using present tense, not past tense. Such errors may reduce a response's overall score. Type out this response to a practice topic. As you type, choose the correct tense at each of the blanks. When you have finished, check your answers on page 73.

Writing Task 1: Writing an Email	27 minutes

ⓘ Read the following information.	**ⓘ In about 150-200 words, write an email to your employee. Your email should do the following things:**
You are a manager at a company. One of your employees has excellent ideas and works hard. However, this person is thinking about quitting work in order to go back to university.	• Say why you think this person is a good worker. • Describe some of the disadvantages of quitting work to attend university. • Mention some benefits of continuing to work at the company.

Dear Mary

I have heard that you are considering quitting your job at this company in order to attend university. I ___1___ **(have been / will be)** impressed with your ideas and with how hard you work. In my view you are an excellent employee, and it ___2___ **(is / will be)** my hope that you will reconsider your plan.

I see several issues with quitting your job. As you ___3___ **(had known / know)**, the economy is not doing well at the moment and few companies ___4___ **(are / were)** hiring new workers. I have read many reports that ___5___ **(had said / say)** this situation will probably continue for a number of years. When you look for work again after going back to university, I am worried that you may find it hard to get a job.

Although many employers want to hire those who have a university education, they ___6___ **(are / were)** often more interested in employing people with relevant work experience. As a result, continuing to work in this job ___7___ **(has given / will give)** you valuable work skills. With improved skills you may get a promotion at this company, or you may find a great position at another company. For these two reasons, I strongly advise you to continue working.

Please come to my office anytime if you ___8___ **(will wish / wish)** to discuss this further.

Robert Smith

Useful Language

These words and phrases may help you write an effective response to a Task 1 writing topic, especially one similar to the topics on this page and pages 22 and 24. There are more useful phrases on page 102.

And second, ...	*Use this phrase to introduce a second point, opinion, problem, and so on; note that including "And" suggests that this is your final point*
First, ...	*Use this word to introduce a first point, opinion, problem, and so on*
For these two reasons, ...	*Use this phrase before you summarize your opinion about a topic or the option you chose*
I have heard that ...	*Use this phrase to introduce some information that you heard from somebody else, read in a newspaper, and so on*
I see two problems with ...	*Use these words to introduce problems or issues with something, such as somebody's plan*
It is my hope that ...	*Use these words as a somewhat formal alternative to "I hope that"*
These days, ...	*Use this phrase to introduce a situation that is currently true*

Challenge Topic 1.2

Type a response to this Writing Task 1 challenge topic in 27 minutes. Use the expert's response on page 23 as a guide. (See page 10 for a suggestion about how to get authentic practice when you type your response.) When you have finished, compare your response to the suggested response on page 75.

Writing Task 1: Writing an Email	27 minutes
ℹ️ **Read the following information.** Your friend is an excellent cook. For many years, your friend has wanted to become a chef. Recently, however, your friend is thinking of giving up this dream and getting a job working in a store.	ℹ️ **In about 150-200 words, write an email to your friend. Your email should do the following things:** • Say why you think your friend is good at cooking. • Describe some of the benefits to your friend of trying to achieve his or her dream. • Mention some disadvantages of finding a job working in a store.

TASK 1: TOPIC 1.3

Topic

> *Read this Writing Task 1 topic. What information in the topic is important?*
> *How could this information help you to write an effective response to the topic?*

Writing Task 1: Writing an Email	27 minutes
ℹ️ **Read the following information.** Every year your whole family spends one day together in the summer. This year, your sister is organizing the day. You want to suggest an activity that you think your family would enjoy.	ℹ️ **In about 150-200 words, write an email to your sister. Your email should do the following things:** • Describe the activity you think the family should do this year. • Give details about where the activity is and how much it costs. • Explain why this activity is good for everybody in your family.

Analysis

> *Read this analysis of the topic by a test expert. Do the expert's ideas about the topic match your ideas?*

The background information describes a situation with your family. From this, you can expect that your email should be informal. Specifically, the background information mentions a regular family event and says that you want to make a suggestion, so you can understand that your email should focus on the benefits of something. This is a common type of email writing task in CELPIP.

The prompt tells you to write to your sister. This tells you that it would be natural to use your sister's name (e.g., "Sue"). Writing to "Dear Sister" or "Dear Sis" might also be possible, or just beginning "Hi."

The prompt also tells you to do three things. First, you have to describe an activity you think your family should do. A good response will include specific details about the activity. To avoid errors, make sure you write about a familiar activity. Second, you have to give details about where this activity is and how much it costs. A good response will be specific (e.g., "It is one hour north of the city by car") rather than general (e.g., "It is outside the city"). Finally, you have to explain why the activity is good for everyone in the family. A good response will mention family members by name and give specific reasons why they would enjoy it.

Expert's Response

Read this response by a test expert and the detailed analysis that explains why it is a good response.

Hi Mary

I hope you and your family are well. Things here are fine.

As you know, our family day is coming soon. I have an idea for something we could do that I think we'd all enjoy. Why don't we spend the day picking apples?

There is an apple farm north of Toronto that lets people pick their own apples on weekends. It's easy to get to the farm by car or by subway and then bus. I went there last year with some friends, and it took only 40 minutes or so. There is no cost to enter, and the apples are just $3 per kilogram, which is much cheaper than most supermarkets.

There are several reasons why I think this would be great. First, everyone in the family loves apples, especially when Mom makes them into an apple pie! And the farm has plenty of fun things for children to do, such as a play area, so all of the kids would have fun, too.

Give me a call so we can discuss further.

Love

Robert

The prompt says to write to your sister, so it is natural to use "Hi" and your sister's first name.

This paragraph does not address any of the bullet points. However, it is natural to include sentences like these in an email to a family member.

In the second paragraph, the writer covers the first bullet in the prompt. Notice how the writer makes the suggestion about what to do in the form of a question. This is very natural.

In the third paragraph, the writer clearly covers the second bullet in the prompt. Notice how the writer gives specific details about the distance to the farm and the cost of the apples. Details like these make the response seem both natural and believable.

In the fourth paragraph, the writer explains why his proposal would be good for the whole family.

This final sentence is a natural way to end an email like this, especially one to a family member.

Using "Love" is a natural way to close an email to a family member. It would probably not be an appropriate way to close an email to a friend, and would definitely not be suitable for an email to anybody else.

Notice how the writer uses only his first name here, which mirrors the greeting.

This response has 179 words, excellent coherence and meaning, good lexical range, high readability and comprehensibility, and great task fulfillment. **Like all responses in this book, it would likely score 11 – 12.**

Practice Topic 1.3

Many test-takers make mistakes with articles (a, an, and the). Such errors may reduce a response's overall score. Type out this response to a practice topic. As you type, add the correct article at each blank. In some cases, no article is needed. When you have finished, check your answers on page 76.

Writing Task 1: Writing an Email	27 minutes

ⓘ Read the following information.	**ⓘ In about 150-200 words, write an email to your friend. Your email should do the following things:**
Every year you and several old friends spend a few days together in the winter. This year, your friend Sam is organizing things. You want to suggest an activity that you think everyone would enjoy.	• Describe the activity you think you and your friends should do this year. • Give details about where the activity is and how much it costs. • Explain why this activity is good for everyone.

Hi Mary

I hope you and your family are well. Things here are fine.

As you know, our old friends' day is coming soon. I have [1_____] idea for something we could do that I think we'd all enjoy. How about going skiing for [2_____] day?

Blue Mountain is [3_____] resort north of Toronto that has some good places to ski. It's easy to get there by car or bus. I went there last year with my family, and it took only two hours or so. There are [4_____] lot of hotels around there that are relatively inexpensive, and [5_____] ski tickets are pretty cheap, too.

There are several reasons why I think this would be great. First, everyone in our group loves skiing, especially when Bob falls over! And [6_____] Blue Mountain has some great shops, restaurants, and nightclubs, too, so we can also enjoy [7_____] evenings and other times when we're not skiing.

Give me [8_____] call so we can discuss further.

Robert

Useful Language

These words and phrases may help you write an effective response to a Task 1 writing topic, especially one similar to the topics on this page and pages 26 and 28. There are more useful phrases on page 102.

As you know, ...	*Use this phrase to introduce some information that the person reading your email already knows*
Give me a call so ...	*Use these words to ask the other person to get in touch with you for a particular reason*
How about ... ?	*Use this phrase to suggest something that you and other people could do; note that the word after "about" should be an –ing word like "going" or "doing"; also note that the sentence should end with a question mark*
I hope you ...	*Use this phrase to express a thing you hope about somebody else*
Inexpensive	*Use this word as a relatively formal alternative to "cheap"*
There are several reasons why ...	*Use this phrase to introduce several reasons for something*
Why don't we ... ?	*Use this phrase to suggest something that you and other people could do; note that the sentence should end with a question mark*

Challenge Topic 1.3

Type a response to this Writing Task 1 challenge topic in 27 minutes. Use the expert's response on page 27 as a guide. (See page 10 for a suggestion about how to get authentic practice when you type your response.) When you have finished, compare your response to the suggested response on page 77.

Writing Task 1: Writing an Email	27 minutes
❶ **Read the following information.**	❶ **In about 150-200 words, write an email to your colleague. Your email should do the following things:**
Every year your company arranges a fun event or trip for all employees. This year, one of your colleagues is in charge of organizing the event. You want to suggest an activity that you think everyone in the company would enjoy.	• Describe the activity you recommend. • Give details about what the activity is. • Explain why this activity is good for everyone in the company.

TASK 1: TOPIC 1.4

Topic

Read this Writing Task 1 topic. What information in the topic is important?
How could this information help you to write an effective response to the topic?

Writing Task 1: Writing an Email	27 minutes
ⓘ Read the following information. You recently saw a boy rescue a dog from a river. Now you have been asked to describe what happened so the story can appear in a local newspaper.	**ⓘ In about 150-200 words, write an email to a reporter at the newspaper. Your email should do the following things:** • Explain where you saw the rescue. • Give details about how and why the dog got into trouble in the river. • Describe how the boy saved the dog and what happened afterwards.

Analysis

Read this analysis of the topic by a test expert. Do the expert's ideas about the topic match your ideas?

The background information describes an event you saw that might be part of the news. From this, you can imagine that your email should be pretty formal. Specifically, the background information tells you that you have to describe a situation you saw in which a boy rescued an animal. Describing events that occurred is a relatively common email writing task in CELPIP.

The prompt tells you to write to a newspaper reporter. It would be most natural to write to "Dear Sir or Madam" or to make up a name for the reporter.

The prompt also tells you to do three things. First, you have to explain where you saw the boy rescue the dog. A good response will include specific details about the location, but you may decide to address this part of the prompt in just one or two sentences. Second, you have to say how and why the dog almost drowned in the river. A good response will give specific details connected sequence words like "First," "then," and "after that." Finally, you have to describe how the boy saved the dog and what happened afterwards. Again, a good response will include specific details and information.

Expert's Response

❚ *Read this response by a test expert and the detailed analysis that explains why it is a good response.*

Dear Sir or Madam

I am writing to tell you about a recent event that I saw when a boy saved a dog from a river.

I was walking home two days ago along the North River near Newtown. I had just passed the Old Bridge when I saw a dog jump into the water. I think the dog was chasing a stick or ball or something like that.

At first it was having fun, but soon the dog seemed to be in trouble. It was trying to swim to the bank of the river but the river was moving very fast, so it could not reach land.

Suddenly, I saw a boy jump into the river. He was a good swimmer, and he quickly reached the dog. He put one arm around the dog and began swimming to the land. He moved slowly, because the dog was heavy, but after a few minutes, he reached the edge of the river. The dog licked the boy's face, and many people clapped their hands and said positive things to the boy.

Please contact me at this email address if you have any questions about what I saw.

Mr R Smith

The writer must write to a newspaper reporter; it is likely the writer does not know the reporter's name, so "Dear Sir or Madam" is a good greeting.

This paragraph does not address any of the bullet points. However, it is often natural to include a sentence that explains your reason for writing.

In the second paragraph, the writer covers the first bullet in the prompt. Notice how the writer gives specific details about where he was and what he saw. This makes the email seem natural.

In the third paragraph, the writer clearly covers the second bullet in the prompt. Again, the writer includes some natural, believable details.

In the fourth paragraph, the writer addresses the last bullet in the prompt. This paragraph is longer than the second and third paragraphs. In general, each paragraph should be about equal in length, but for this topic, the last paragraph is longer as the final bullet requires more information.

This final sentence is a natural way to end an email like this. Notice how the writer says "at this email address." Because all emails automatically include the sender's email address, there is no need for the writer to include his email address in the body of the message.

If you start an email with "Dear Sir or Madam," it is natural to close with just your family name or your initial and then your family name, as here.

This response has 199 words, excellent coherence and meaning, good lexical range, high readability and comprehensibility, and great task fulfillment. **Like all responses in this book, it would likely score 11 – 12.**

Practice Topic 1.4

Many test-takers make small grammar, vocabulary, or punctuation mistakes. Such errors may reduce a response's overall score. Type out this response to a practice topic. As you type, correct each of the underlined mistakes. When you have finished, check your answers on page 78.

Writing Task 1: Writing an Email	27 minutes

ⓘ Read the following information.

You recently saw a police officer prevent a woman from being hit by a car. Your friend has asked you to describe what you saw.

ⓘ In about 150-200 words, write an email to your friend. Your email should do the following things:

- Explain where you saw the police officer help the woman.
- Give details about how and why the woman almost got hit by a car.
- Describe how the police officer helped the woman and what happened afterwards.

Hi Mary

I hope you and your family are well. Things here are fine. As you requested, <u>I write</u> to tell you about a situation I saw <u>the another day</u>.

I was walking home <u>two days before</u> along the North River near Newtown. I had just passed the Old Bridge <u>when I see</u> a woman jogging. She was <u>listening loud music</u> and wearing <u>the dark sunglasses</u>.

As I watched her, she suddenly turned and started to run across the road. A truck was driving towards her <u>very quick</u>, and the driver used his horn to warn her. However, <u>because of</u> she was wearing sunglasses and headphones, I think the woman did not see or hear him.

Suddenly, I saw a police officer run towards the woman. She pushed the woman out of the way of the truck and then jumped out of the way herself. The jogging woman fell over, but she was not hurt by the fall or by <u>a truck</u>. She thanked the police officer <u>many of times</u> for saving her life.

Give me a call if you any questions about what I saw.

Robert

Useful Language

These words and phrases may help you write an effective response to a Task 1 writing topic, especially one similar to the topics on this page and pages 30 and 32. There are more useful phrases on page 102.

As you requested, ...	*Use this phrase to introduce some information that somebody has asked you to give*
At first, ...	*Use these words to say what happened or how something was at the beginning; contrast these words with a phrase like "but soon ..." or "after a while ..."*
However, ...	*Use this word to introduce some contrasting information*
I am writing to tell you about ...	*Use this phrase to explain your reason for writing to somebody*
or something like that	*Use these words to make it clear that you cannot remember something exactly, or did not see something clearly; for example, you might say the cost was "$50 or something like that."*
Please contact me / Give me a call if you have any questions ...	*Use either of these phrases to let the person reading your email know that he or she can get in touch with you for more details.*

Challenge Topic 1.4

Type a response to this Writing Task 1 challenge topic in 27 minutes. Use the expert's response on page 31 as a guide. (See page 10 for a suggestion about how to get authentic practice when you type your response.) When you have finished, compare your response to the suggested response on page 79.

Writing Task 1: Writing an Email	**27 minutes**
ℹ Read the following information. You recently went on a business trip. During your trip, you saw a demonstration of a new computer. Your boss thinks the computer might be useful for your company. Your boss wants you to describe what you saw.	**ℹ In about 150-200 words, write an email to your boss. Your email should do the following things:** • Explain where you saw the demonstration. • Give details about what the computer is like and what it can do. • Say whether you think the computer would be useful for your company, and why.

TASK 1: TOPIC 1.5

Topic

> Read this Writing Task 1 topic. What information in the topic is important?
> How could this information help you to write an effective response to the topic?

Writing Task 1: Writing an Email	27 minutes
ℹ Read the following information. You recently stayed at a hotel for a few nights. The staff at the hotel were excellent and took very good care of you. It was the best service you have ever received at a hotel.	**ℹ In about 150-200 words, write an email to the hotel manager. Your email should do the following things:** • Explain when you stayed at the hotel, for how long, and why. • Give examples of the service you received. • State how you feel about the hotel and its staff.

Analysis

> Read this analysis of the topic by a test expert. Do the expert's ideas about the topic match your ideas?

The background information describes a positive situation. Specifically, it describes a great experience you had at a hotel. From this, you can understand that you will need to give positive examples. Writing an email to say thank you for a positive experience is a relatively common type of email writing task in CELPIP.

The prompt tells you to write to a hotel manager. From this you can understand that you should write a relatively formal email that is addressed to "Dear Sir or Madam" or "Dear Hotel Manager" because most people would not know or find out the manager's actual name.

The prompt also tells you to do three things. First, you have to explain when, why, and for how long you stayed at the hotel. A good response will mention all three pieces of information clearly and give supporting details as necessary. You do not have to describe a real hotel, but it may help you think of supporting details if you write about an actual hotel you have stayed at. Second, you have to give examples of the service you received. Notice that the prompt asks you for "some examples." A good response will include at least two examples with details. Finally, you have to express how you feel about the hotel and its staff. A good response will make it clear that the writer is very thankful and satisfied. Be careful to avoid repetition: one or two sentences may be enough to cover this part of the prompt.

Expert's Response

Read this response by a test expert and the detailed analysis that explains why it is a good response.

Dear Sir or Madam

Last week I had to go to Boston on business. After reading some reviews online, I decided to stay at your hotel from Monday to Wednesday night. I am so happy about my decision because I received such great service.

When I arrived on Monday evening, I was late and hungry because of a delayed flight. The young woman working at the front desk arranged for dinner to be sent to my room despite the kitchen being closed. In addition, when I left the hotel on Thursday morning, I forgot several items. One of your friendly maids followed me out of the hotel and gave them to me just before I got into a taxi to go to the airport. When I tried to give her a tip, she refused and said she was just happy to help.

I can honestly say that your staff provided wonderful service, and I would like to thank you and everyone who works at the hotel. I will definitely stay at your hotel again the next time I visit Boston, and I will recommend your hotel to all of my friends and colleagues, too.

Yours

Mr Robert Smith

The writer must write to a hotel manager. It is likely the writer does not know the manager's name, so "Dear Sir or Madam" is a good greeting.

This paragraph clearly addresses the first bullet in the prompt with specific details. The last sentence in the paragraph summarizes the writer's overall opinion and indirectly explains why he is writing.

The second paragraph covers the second bullet in the prompt. The details that the writer gives are clear and believable. The writer's use of language is clear and simple, too. This means that his response will be easy for the rater to follow. (It also means the response is an excellent model for people who are not native speakers to copy.)

In the third paragraph, the writer clearly covers the third bullet in the prompt. Again, the writer includes some natural, believable details. The final sentence is not mentioned in the prompt, but it is a natural thing to say in an email thanking somebody for excellent service.

The closing phrase is simple but natural. It would also be possible to say something like "Yours sincerely," "Yours faithfully," or "Yours truly."

Because the writer has stayed at the hotel before, it is natural for him to include his first name as well as his family name. However, giving only his family name would also be OK.

This response has 199 words, excellent coherence and meaning, good lexical range, high readability and comprehensibility, and great task fulfillment. **Like all responses in this book, it would likely score 11 – 12.**

Practice Topic 1.5

> *Using adverbs to modify verbs and adjectives is an effective and easy way to make your response longer and more natural. Type out this response to a practice topic. As you type, choose the adverb (or adverbs) that could complete each blank. When you have finished, check your answers on page 79.*

Writing Task 1: Writing an Email	27 minutes

❶ Read the following information.	**❶ In about 150-200 words, write an email to the cruise ship company. Your email should do the following things:**
You recently took a short cruise vacation with your family. The staff on the ship were excellent and took very good care of you. It was the best vacation you have ever taken.	<ul><li>Explain when you went on the cruise, for how long, and where.</li><li>Give some examples of the service you received.</li><li>State how you feel about the ship and its staff.</li></ul>

Dear Sir or Madam

Last month my family and I took a five-night cruise vacation with your company. We travelled in Europe from Norway south to the United Kingdom. We are [1] _____ (so / usually / very) happy about our decision to take a vacation with your company because we received great service and had a wonderful time.

When we arrived in Norway, a young woman from your staff was at the airport to greet us. Our hotel lost our reservation, but she helped us sort the problem out [2] _____ (effectively / quickly / really) and easily. Next day she drove us and several other families to the cruise ship. While we were enjoying the cruise, the great service continued from [3] _____ (almost / nearly / totally) every member of staff. In addition, we were [4] _____ (incredibly / mostly / really) happy with the wonderful food and the excellent activities and entertainment. All in all, it was [5] _____ (closely / truly / very) a fantastic trip.

I can [6] _____ (honestly / nearly / totally) say that your staff provided wonderful service, and I would like to thank you and everybody who works on your cruise ship. Everyone in my family wants to take another cruise with your company next year, and I will definitely recommend you to my friends and colleagues, too.

Yours

Mr Robert Smith

Useful Language

These words and phrases may help you write an effective response to a Task 1 writing topic, especially one similar to the topics on this page and pages 34 and 36. There are more useful phrases on page 102.

I can honestly say that …	*Use these words when you wish to express a strong, honest opinion about something*
I will definitely …	*Use these words to introduce something that you are certain you will do in the future*
I will recommend …	*Use these words to introduce something that you will suggest to other people*
I would like to thank you …	*Use these words to introduce something that you would like to say thank you to other people for*
In addition, …	*Use this phrase to introduce a second or third point*
sort (the problem) out	*Use this phrasal verb to describe solving or fixing a problem; note that both "sort a problem out" and "sort out a problem" are both correct English; also note that you can "sort out a problem" or "an issue" or "a situation" and so on.*

Challenge Topic 1.5

Type a response to this Writing Task 1 challenge topic in 27 minutes. Use the expert's response on page 35 as a guide. (See page 10 for a suggestion about how to get authentic practice when you type your response.) When you have finished, compare your response to the suggested response on page 81.

Writing Task 1: Writing an Email	27 minutes
ℹ Read the following information.	**ℹ In about 150-200 words, write an email to the hotel manager. Your email should do the following things:**
You recently stayed at a hotel for a few nights. The staff at the hotel were unprofessional and did not provide you with good care. It was the worst service you have ever received at a hotel.	• Explain when you stayed at the hotel, for how long, and why. • Give some examples of the service you received. • State how you feel about the hotel and its staff.

TASK 1: ADDITIONAL TOPICS

Use these five additional topics to get more writing practice for Task 1. You will get the most benefit if you write under test conditions. This means typing each response in 27 minutes. (The study tip on page 10 explains how to use a free online CELPIP test to get an authentic experience when typing your responses.)

Additional Topic 1.6

A sample response to this topic written by a test expert is on page 82.

Writing Task 1: Writing an Email	27 minutes
ⓘ Read the following information. You volunteer at a local hospital for children. Your manager has asked you to contact local businesses to raise money for new equipment to save children's lives.	**ⓘ In about 150-200 words, write an email to a local company. Your email should do the following things:** • Explain who you are and why you are writing. • Describe how the hospital will use any money that is raised. • Say how much money you need and how the company can donate it

Additional Topic 1.7

A sample response to this topic written by a test expert is on page 83.

Writing Task 1: Writing an Email	27 minutes
ⓘ Read the following information. Every day you take lunch to work and leave it in a refrigerator at your office. For the last few days, somebody has been eating part of your lunch.	**ⓘ In about 150-200 words, write an email to your co-workers. Your email should do the following things:** • Explain why you bring lunch every day and what your lunch looks like. • Say what has been happening for the last few days and how it makes you feel. • Describe what you will do if somebody continues to eat items of food from your lunch.

Additional Topic 1.8

A sample response to this topic written by a test expert is on page 84.

Writing Task 1: Writing an Email	27 minutes

ℹ Read the following information.	**ℹ In about 150-200 words, write an email to the manager of the restaurant. Your email should do the following things:**
You recently went out for dinner at a popular and expensive restaurant near your home. It was not a good experience: the service was average, the food was poor, and you were charged too much. Neither the chef nor the restaurant manager was available to help you.	• Explain when you went to the restaurant, why, and what you expected. • Give examples of the problems you experienced while eating there. • Suggest how the manager could fix the issues to your satisfaction.

Additional Topic 1.9

A sample response to this topic written by a test expert is on page 85.

Writing Task 1: Writing an Email	27 minutes

ℹ Read the following information.	**ℹ In about 150-200 words, write an email to the person organizing the hiking group. Your email should do the following things:**
You saw a poster at the library about a new hiking group that is starting in your area. You love hiking and would like to join this group.	• Say who you are and why you would like to join the hiking group. • Ask how you can become a member and how often the group will meet. • Suggest some places you have previously been that are good for hiking.

Additional Topic 1.10

A sample response to this topic written by a test expert is on page 86.

Writing Task 1: Writing an Email	27 minutes

🛈 **Read the following information.**	🛈 **In about 150-200 words, write an email to the store manager. Your email should do the following things:**
You recently shopped at a store that is two hours from your home by car. When you got home, you realized that the store charged you too much. You called the store, but were told you had to return in person to have the extra charge corrected.	• Say which items you were overcharged for. • Explain why you do not wish to return to the store in person. • Suggest what actions the manager could take to solve the problem.

Suggestions for Finding Additional Practice Topics

Here are some suggestions for creating and finding additional writing topics for Task 1.

1. Create your own topics by making small changes to the topics in this book

It is relatively easy to come up with new topics by making small changes to the topics in this book (or other books). Look at Writing Challenge 1.1 on page 21. Notice how Challenge 1.1 changes the original topic slightly so that instead of writing about how noise from a building site disturbs you, you have to write about noise from a nightclub. Also notice how Writing Challenge 1.5 on page 37 asks you to write about the opposite of the original prompt: instead of praising great service, you have to complain about poor service.

2. Borrow or purchase official CELPIP writing questions

Paragon Testing Enterprises is the organization that develops and administers the CELPIP Test. This organization sells official practice tests and study materials for CELPIP. You may be able to borrow these from the library or purchase them online from this website: https://www.paragontesting.ca/

3. Use Writing Task 1 questions from study materials for the IELTS General test

The first writing task in IELTS General is very similar to the Writing Task 1 in CELPIP. You may be able to borrow study materials for IELTS General from a library. (Note that only Writing Task 1 in IELTS General is useful for CELPIP; practicing Writing Task 1 from IELTS Academic would *not* help you for CELPIP.)

TASK 2: INTRODUCTION

After your time for Task 1 ends, or after you choose to finish Task 1 early, the computer will go on to Task 2. When Task 2 begins, the screen will look something like this:

Writing Task 2: Responding to Survey Questions Time remaining: 25 minutes 43 seconds

ℹ Read the following information.

Office Location

Your company is planning to move to a new location. Your manager is considering two locations and wants to know your views. One location would be a larger office in the suburbs 30 minutes away from the city that has a lot of space for employees, but which clients cannot visit easily. The other location is a smaller office in the centre of the city with less space for workers, but which clients could visit easily.

ℹ Choose the option that you prefer. Explain the reasons for your choice. Why do you prefer it? Write about 150-200 words.

○ **Option A:** Large Suburban Office: The company will pay $10,000 in rent per month.

○ **Option B:** Small Downtown Office: The company will pay $20,000 in rent per month.

At the top of the screen, you will see the title bar, which explains which writing task you are currently responding to, and how much time you have left. For Task 2, you have 26 minutes in total. When the time is up, the computer will automatically save your responses and move on to the Speaking Test.

Writing Task 2: Responding to Survey Questions Time remaining: 25 minutes 43 seconds

---

ℹ Read the following information.

Office Location

Your company is planning to move to a new location. Your manager is considering two locations and wants to know your views. One location would be a larger office in the suburbs 30 minutes away from the city that has a lot of space for employees, but which clients cannot visit easily. The other location is a smaller office in the centre of the city with less space for workers, but which clients could visit easily.

On the left of the screen, you will see some background information. This information describes a situation. You will need to read this information to understand the task.

The background information often mentions who has asked you for your opinion, but in most cases, this information is not useful.

On the right of the screen, you will see the prompt. This explains what information your response should include. In general, the prompt will ask you to do two things: explain which option you prefer, and why. In some cases, the prompt will also ask you to discuss any problems with the other option.

You will see the options below the prompt, usually labelled Option A and Option B. Each option will also have a short title, and a description. This description is will help you make choose the option you prefer; it will also help you write an effective response.

ℹ Choose the option that you prefer. Explain the reasons for your choice. Why do you prefer it? Write about 150-200 words.

O **Option A:** Large Suburban Office: The company will pay $10,000 in rent per month.

O **Option B:** Small Downtown Office: The company will pay $20,000 in rent per month.

The white box below the prompt is where you should type your response. As you type, a scroll bar will appear so that you can see your whole response. You will see the word count below the white box.

As a general rule, a good response to Writing Task 2 will include these elements:

- An introduction that briefly states which option you prefer.

- Two or three body paragraphs that each give a reason why you prefer your chosen option. Each reason should be supported with details or an example. It is often a good idea to discuss any problems with the other option, too, even if the prompt does not specifically ask you to do this.

- A conclusion that summarizes your preference.

TASK 2: ANALYSIS OF A RESPONSE

Read the prompt and response by a test expert on this page. Then read the analysis of the response on the next page. This will help you understand how to write effective, high-scoring responses to Task 2 prompts.

Writing Task 2: Responding to Survey Questions　　　　Time remaining: 25 minutes 43 seconds

ℹ Read the following information.

Office Location

Your company is planning to move to a new location. Your manager is considering two locations and wants to know your views. One location would be a larger office in the suburbs 30 minutes away from the city that has a lot of space for employees, but which clients cannot visit easily. The other location is a smaller office in the centre of the city with less space for workers, but which clients could visit easily.

ℹ Choose the option that you prefer. Explain the reasons for your choice. Why do you prefer it? Write about 150-200 words.

○ **Option A:** Large Suburban Office: The company will pay $10,000 in rent per month.

○ **Option B:** Small Downtown Office: The company will pay $20,000 in rent per month.

Both options have some advantages, and I can see why some might prefer Option A. If I had to make a choice, however, there are several reasons why I would go for Option B.

The main reason is that a small downtown office would be more convenient for clients to visit. Without clients the company might not be profitable and could have to close. Therefore, I think the company should do everything it can to give clients not the best service. In my view, forcing them to travel to an inconvenient, suburban location would not achieve this aim.

Of course, the limited space and high cost are two disadvantages of Option B. However, having extra space for employees would not help them work more efficiently. And the company could easily afford the monthly rent of $20,000 if it could attract one or two new clients per month.

So for the reasons that I have outlined, I feel Option A is the better choice.

Both options have some advantages, and I can see why some might prefer Option A. If I had to make a choice, however, there are several reasons why I would go for Option B.

The main reason is that a small downtown office would be more convenient for clients to visit. Without clients the company might not be profitable and could have to close. Therefore, I think the company should do everything it can to give clients not the best service. In my view, forcing them to travel to an inconvenient, suburban location would not achieve this aim.

Of course, the limited space and high cost are two disadvantages of Option B. However, having extra space for employees would not help them work more efficiently. And the company could easily afford the monthly rent of $20,000 if it could attract one or two new clients per month.

So for the reasons that I have outlined, I feel Option A is the better choice.

Every survey response should begin with an introductory paragraph. The introduction should clearly state which of the two options you prefer.

In most cases, survey responses will need two or three body paragraph. In this case, the writer decides to use two body paragraphs. In the first body paragraph, the writer gives one advantage of his preferred option. Notice the writer's use of words and phrases that suggest conditional possibility rather than certainty, such as "would be" or "might not be."

In the second body paragraph, the writer mentions some disadvantages of his preferred option and how the company could overcome these disadvantages, so it is still clear why he favours Option B. And again, notice the conditional language that the writer uses.

It is not necessary to have a concluding paragraph in the survey response, but it will increase the length of your response and make it seem well balanced. If you do add a conclusion, it should summarize your reasons and opinion, as this conclusion does.

This response, which has 163 words, is clearly organized, well written, and addresses the task fully. Its only weakness is that the language is deliberately somewhat simple in places. **It would probably score 11 – 12.**

TASK 2: STEP-BY-STEP GUIDE

Writing Task 2 questions follow a standard pattern. As a result, you can follow the same steps each time you write a Task 2 response either for practice or during the official CELPIP test.

Step 1

Read the background information carefully. Look for useful information that will help you understand your task. For example, is the survey about a work situation, about the place where you live, or about something else? (In most cases, it will be about a work situation.)

Next read the prompt and the two options carefully, and decide which option you prefer. (You can wait until Step 2 to make this decision, if you prefer to brainstorm first.)

Step 2

After carefully reading the background information and prompt, you should brainstorm ideas.

When you brainstorm, you should:

- Think of ideas, supporting details, and examples that match either the background information or the option that you prefer

(If you wish, you can also brainstorm words and grammar structures that would be natural to use when you type your response to the prompt.)

If you wish, you can make a note of your ideas on a piece of paper. This is not necessary, but it will help you remember your ideas when you are typing your response, so it is usually a good idea to do this.

Step 2 *continued*

For example, for the Topic 2.1 shown on page 48, you might brainstorm and note down ideas like these:

- Option B
    = everyone arrives on time
        → no problem with late people
    = people can relax and enjoy party
        → no problem if people eat / drink a lot
    = people can chat while going to party
        → not possible with option A

After brainstorming and deciding which of your ideas to write about, you also need to decide how best to organize your response. Typically, this will depend on how many reasons with examples you have thought of to support your preference.

For example, if you came up with two reasons and examples, you should probably include an introduction, two body paragraphs (one for each reason), and a conclusion. However, if you came up with three reasons each with examples, it might be better to organize your response with an introduction, three body paragraphs (one for each reason), and a conclusion.

Note that if you have two or three reasons that are on the same theme – for example, two reasons that are both related to money, or three reasons that are all connected with time – you may wish to have an introduction, a single longer body paragraph, and a conclusion. You can see an example of this in the response to Topic 2.5 on page 64.

Plan to spend up to five minutes on Step 2, but do it more quickly if you can.

Test Expert Writing Practice *for* **CELPIP**®

Step 3

After brainstorming your ideas, you need to type your response. (Remember: you will not be able to write your response by hand.) When you type, you should follow the organization you decided on in Step 2 and write about the reasons you thought of in Step 2.

As you type each sentence, focus on the following things:

- Be careful about mistakes, especially basic mistakes like forgetting to put -s or -ed on the ends of words, or using the wrong tense. Mistakes like these are likely to reduce your score.

- Avoid writing sentences that are too long because these are likely to confuse the rater, which may affect your score. As a rule, sentences up to 20 words long are generally OK.

- Do not use too many simple sentences – good responses usually have a balance of simple, compound, and complex sentences. (If you are not sure what these terms mean, check a grammar book or look up the information online.)

- In your introduction and conclusion, make sure each sentence is clearly relevant to the topic and to your preferred option.

- In your body paragraphs, make sure each sentence either expresses your preference, gives a reason for your preference, adds information that supports your preference, or discusses problems with the option that you do not prefer.

Spend as much time as you need on Step 3. Do NOT try to save time at the end; it is better to write a full response than to write a shorter one just so you have a few minutes left at the end.

Step 4

If you have any time left at the end, try to improve your response by doing one of these things:

- Check you have used clear connectors (e.g., *As a result*) and sequence words (e.g., *Firstly*).

- Look for opportunities to add details or examples to make your ideas and points clearer.

- Fix any mistakes that you notice. (But keep in mind that you will probably not be able to fix all of your mistakes; as a result, fixing mistakes is unlikely to affect your overall score.)

TASK 2: TOPIC 2.1

Topic

> *Read this Writing Task 2 topic. What information in the topic is important?*
> *How could this information help you to write an effective response to the topic?*

Writing Task 2: Responding to Survey Questions	26 minutes
ⓘ Read the following information. **Office Party Transportation** Your company is planning a party to celebrate the end of the year. The party will take place at a location about one hour outside of town. The person organizing the party wants your opinion about the best way for employees to travel to the location of the party.	**ⓘ Choose the option that you prefer. Explain the reasons for your choice. Why do you prefer your choice? Write about 150-200 words.** O **Option A:** Individual Transportation: Workers should use their own transportation to travel to the place where the party will be held. O **Option B:** Group Transportation: The company should arrange transportation to take workers to the place where the party will be held.

Analysis

> *Read this analysis of the topic by a test expert. Do the expert's ideas about the topic match your ideas?*

The background information describes a work situation. This is the most common type of Task 2 situation that you will see in CELPIP. In this case, the background information explains that your company is hosting a party for workers and wants to know your views on transportation.

The prompt asks you to choose one option, and explain why this is your choice. It does not specifically ask you to discuss problems with the other choice, but you can do this, if you wish. The first option is for workers to use their own transportation to get to the party. The second option is for the company to arrange transportation for all workers. Remember that neither option is better than the other, and the raters will judge your response based on the quality of your writing, not based on which option you chose. A good response will give at least two clear reasons why one option is better than the other. These could be reasons that are true only for you, or reasons that are true for you and other workers.

Expert's Response

Read this response by a test expert and the detailed analysis that explains why it is a good response.

Both options have some advantages, and I can see why some of my colleagues might choose Option A. On the whole, however, there are several reasons why Option B would be my preference.

This introductory paragraph begins by stating that both options have advantages. In the final sentence, the writer states his preferred option using natural language.

For one thing, if the company were to arrange transportation, everybody would arrive on time and nobody would get lost. At past office parties, some people who travelled on their own have been late. This caused the people who arrived on time to get frustrated while waiting for them.

In the first body paragraph, the writer gives one reason why he thinks Option B is better than Option A. He supports this reason with a detailed and believable example that refers to previous events that were similar. This is an effective way to support one's opinion about something.

For another thing, if people know they do not have to drive themselves, they can relax and enjoy the celebration more. They can eat and drink whatever they like without worrying. In contrast, people travelling to the party in their own cars might not enjoy the party because of concern about driving home after it finished.

In the second body paragraph, the writer gives a second reason why he thinks Option B is better. Again, he supports his reason with an example that shows a disadvantage of the other option.

Finally, if the company arranges transportation for everyone, people can chat with each other on the way to and from the party. This will promote good feelings and help the party to be a big success. If a lot of people were travelling to the party on their own, however, this would not be possible.

In the third body paragraph, the writer gives a final reason why Option B is his preference. Like the earlier body paragraphs, he supports his view with an example that shows a disadvantage of the other option.

So as far as I am concerned, Option B is the better choice.

The concluding paragraph sums up the writer's opinion and explicitly states his preference.

This response has 206 words, excellent coherence and meaning, good lexical range, high readability and comprehensibility, and great task fulfillment. **Like all responses in this book, it would likely score 11 – 12.**

Practice Topic 2.1

Type out this response to a practice topic. As you type, complete the blanks in your own words. Use the response on page 49 as a guide. Then compare your completed response with the one on page 87.

Writing Task 2: Responding to Survey Questions	26 minutes

❶ **Read the following information.**	❶ **Choose the option that you prefer. Explain the reasons for your choice. Why do you prefer your choice? Write about 150-200 words.**
Transportation to Training Session Your company is holding a special training session for all senior employees next week. The training will take place at a location about one hour away from the office. The person organizing the training wants your opinion about the best way for staff to travel to the training location.	○ **Option A:** Individual Transportation: Workers should use their own transportation to travel to the training session. ○ **Option B:** Group Transportation: The company should arrange transportation to take staff to the training session.

Both options have some advantages, and [1   ]. On the whole, however, there are several reasons why Option B would be my preference.

For one thing, if the company were to arrange transportation, [2   ]. At past training sessions, some people who travelled on their own have been late. This caused the people who arrived on time to become frustrated while waiting for them.

For another thing, if people know they do not have to drive themselves, [3   ]. In contrast, people travelling to the training session in their own cars might not be able to concentrate because of concern about driving home in heavy traffic after it finished.

Finally, if the company arranges transportation for everyone, people can chat with each other on the way to and from the session. [4   ]. If a lot of people were travelling to the training on their own, however, this would not be possible.

So as far as I am concerned, Option B is the better choice.

Useful Language

These words and phrases may help you write an effective response to a Task 2 writing topic, especially one similar to the topics on this page and pages 48 and 50. There are more useful phrases on page 102.

As far as I am concerned, ...	*Use this phrase to introduce your opinion about something; note that this phrase sounds especially natural if other people might hold an alternative opinion*
Both options have some advantages, ...	*Use these words to make it clear that you believe two choices both have benefits*
For one thing, ...	*Use this phrase to introduce one point or reason for your opinion*
For another thing, ...	*Use this phrase to introduce a second point or reason for your view*
Finally, ...	*Use this phrase to introduce a final point or reason for your view*
On the whole, ...	*Use this phrase to introduce your opinion about something; note that this phrase suggests you think another view has some benefits*

Challenge Topic 2.1

Type a response to this Writing Task 2 challenge topic in 26 minutes. Use the expert's response on page 49 as a guide. (See page 10 for a suggestion about how to get authentic practice when you type your response.) When you have finished, compare your response to the suggested response on page 88.

Writing Task 2: Responding to Survey Questions	26 minutes
❶ **Read the following information.** **Transportation to Meeting** Your company is holding a meeting for many staff members next month. The meeting will take place in another city. The person organizing the meeting wants to know whether employees prefer to travel to this city by train or by bus.	❶ **Choose the option that you prefer. Explain the reasons for your choice. Why do you prefer your choice? Write about 150-200 words.** ○ **Option A:** Train: The journey takes five hours. Employees arrive in the other city at 9 PM. ○ **Option B:** Bus: The journey takes nine hours. Employees travel overnight and arrive in the other city at 6 AM.

TASK 2: TOPIC 2.2

Topic

Read this Writing Task 2 topic. What information in the topic is important?
How could this information help you to write an effective response to the topic?

Writing Task 2: Responding to Survey Questions	26 minutes
ℹ Read the following information. **Reward for Employees** Your company has been successful recently, and your manager wants to reward everyone. One option is to give employees a transportation pass that would allow free use of public transit for six months. The second option is to give employees a financial bonus equal to half their regular monthly salary. Your manager wants to know your views.	**ℹ Choose the option that you prefer. Explain the reasons for your choice. Why do you prefer it? What problems are there with the other choice? Write about 150-200 words.** O **Option A:** Transportation Pass: You would not have to pay any tax if you get the pass. O **Option B:** Financial Bonus: You would have to pay tax on the bonus amount if you receive the financial bonus.

Analysis

Read this analysis of the topic by a test expert. Do the expert's ideas about the topic match your ideas?

The background information describes a work situation. This is the most common type of Task 2 situation that you will see in CELPIP. In this case, the background information explains that your company wants to reward employees and asks workers for their views about which of two rewards is more attractive. The background information gives details about the rewards that the prompt does not mention. For example, it explains that the transit pass is valid for six months. A good response will include this kind of information.

The prompt asks you to choose one option, and explain why this is your choice. It specifically asks you to discuss problems with the other choice, too. If you do not do this, your score will be affected. The first option is for workers to receive a transportation pass. The second option is for workers to get a financial bonus. Remember that neither option is better than the other, and the raters will judge your response based on the quality of your writing, not based on which option you chose. A good response will give at least two clear reasons why one option is better than the other. These could be reasons that are true only for you, or reasons that are true for other workers.

Expert's Response

Read this response by a test expert and the detailed analysis that explains why it is a good response.

Both options have some advantages, and I can see why some of my colleagues might prefer Option A. If I had to make a choice, however, there are several reasons why I would go for Option B.

This introductory paragraph begins by suggesting that Option A has advantages. In the final sentence, the writer makes his preference clear using natural, conditional language.

On the one hand, as far as I know only about 50 percent or so of people who work at the office use public transportation to commute to work. Everyone else comes to the office by car, by bike, or on foot. This means that about half of all employees would not find the six-month transit pass particularly useful. Of course, they could use the pass in other ways, not just for commuting to work, but it is still not a very useful reward for them.

In the first body paragraph, the writer gives one reason why he thinks Option A is not as good as Option B. He supports this reason with details. The use of statistics – like "50 percent or so" and "about half of all" – is especially effective. Note that the writer does not explicitly state that his preference is Option B in this paragraph, but this is obvious from the way he says that the Option A reward is "not a very useful" one.

On the other hand, if employees were to get a financial bonus, all of them would benefit depending on their needs or wishes. I expect some would choose to spend the extra money on regular expenses, such as bills or groceries. Others might purchase a luxury item, such as a new television or a tablet computer. And still others might use the money for a short vacation. In other words, a financial bonus would give employees more choice.

In the second body paragraph, the writer explains why he thinks Option B is better than Option A. Again, he supports his reason with details and examples. In the final sentence, he sums up the main benefit of Option B: it gives people "more choice."

So for the reasons that I have outlined, I feel Option B is the better choice.

The concluding paragraph sums up the writer's opinion and explicitly states his preference.

This response has 217 words, excellent coherence and meaning, good lexical range, high readability and comprehensibility, and great task fulfillment. **Like all responses in this book, it would likely score 11 – 12.**

Practice Topic 2.2

Type out this response to a practice topic. As you type, complete the blanks in your own words. Use the response on page 53 as a guide. Then compare your completed response with the one on page 89.

Writing Task 2: Responding to Survey Questions	26 minutes

ℹ **Read the following information.** **Reward for Employees** Your company has been successful recently, and your manager wants to reward everyone. One option is to hold a large party for all employees. The second option is to give all employees one extra day off. Your manager wants to know what you think.	ℹ **Choose the option that you prefer. Explain the reasons for your choice. Why do you prefer it? What problems are there with the other choice? Write about 150-200 words.** ○ **Option A:** Party for Employees: The party would be held on a Saturday or Sunday. ○ **Option B:** Extra Day Off: Employees would have to use the extra day off within six weeks.

Both options have some advantages, and I can see why some of my co-workers might prefer Option A. ⬚1 .

On the one hand, a party would be fun and a nice way to celebrate the company's success. However, the company already hosts a summer picnic, which is coming up soon, and having two events for staff so close together seems unnecessary. And because the party would be held on a Saturday or Sunday, ⬚2 .

On the other hand, if employees were to get an extra day off, ⬚3 . I expect some would choose to spend the day doing regular things like shopping or doing work around the home. Others might combine the extra day with some vacation days and take a short trip somewhere nice. And still others ⬚4 . In other words, an extra day off would give employees more choice.

So for the reasons that I have outlined, ⬚5 .

Useful Language

I can see why some ...	*Use these words to introduce an opinion that some people might hold about something*
If I had to make a choice, ...	*Use this phrase to express a choice about a hypothetical situation*
Of course, ...	*Use this phrase when you want to say something that most people would consider to be obvious*
On the one hand, ...	*Use this phrase to introduce one idea that will be contrast with another idea that you later introduce with "On the other hand".*
On the other hand, ...	*Use this phrase to introduce a second idea that contrasts with an earlier idea you introduced with "On the one hand".*
This means that ...	*Use these words either to clarify the meaning of an idea you have just mentioned, or to talk about the result of something.*

Challenge Topic 2.2

Type a response to this Writing Task 2 challenge topic in 26 minutes. Use the expert's response on page 53 as a guide. (See page 10 for a suggestion about how to get authentic practice when you type your response.) When you have finished, compare your response to the suggested response on page 90.

Writing Task 2: Responding to Survey Questions	26 minutes
ℹ **Read the following information.** **Financial Bonus from Your City** The city where you live recently received a large sum of money from the government. The city council will use the money to benefit local people. One option is to give every resident, excluding children, a small sum of money. The other option is to give taxpayers a tax rebate.	ℹ **Choose the option that you prefer. Explain the reasons for your choice. Why do you prefer it? What problems are there with the other choice? Write about 150-200 words.** O **Option A:** Money: Each adult resident of the city would get $500 immediately. O **Option B:** Tax Rebate: All taxpayers would get a rebate worth up to $600 at the end of the year.

TASK 2: TOPIC 2.3

Topic

Read this Writing Task 2 topic. What information in the topic is important?
How could this information help you to write an effective response to the topic?

Writing Task 2: Responding to Survey Questions	26 minutes
ⓘ Read the following information. **Apartment Building Improvements** You live in a large apartment building. The building owner is planning to improve the building either by adding a large function room that residents could reserve to hold meetings or have events, or by adding a modern fitness centre. The owner has asked all residents of the building to fill out an opinion survey.	**ⓘ Choose the option that you prefer. Explain the reasons for your choice. Why do you prefer it? Write about 150-200 words.** O **Option A:** Function Room: The function room would have enough space to hold events for up to 80 people. O **Option B:** Fitness Centre: The fitness centre would be free to use by up to 12 residents at one time.

Analysis

Read this analysis of the topic by a test expert. Do the expert's ideas about the topic match your ideas?

The background information describes a situation related to where you live. This is a relatively common Task 2 situation in CELPIP. In this case, the background information explains that the owner of the apartment building where you live wants the opinion of residents about how to improve the building.

The prompt asks you to choose one option, and explain why this is your choice. It does not specifically ask you to discuss problems with the other choice, but you can do this, if you wish.

The first option is for the building owner to add a function room that residents can reserve for events. The second option is for the building owner to add a fitness centre. Remember that neither option is better than the other, and the raters will judge your response based on the quality of your writing, not based on which option you chose. A good response will give at least two clear reasons why one option is better than the other. These could be reasons that are true only for you, or reasons that are true for other people who live in your building.

Expert's Response

Read this response by a test expert and the detailed analysis that explains why it is a good response.

Both options have some advantages, and I can see why some building residents might choose Option B. On the whole, however, there are several reasons why Option A would be my preference.

This introductory paragraph begins by stating that both options have advantages. In the final sentence, the writer states his preferred option using natural language.

Firstly, there are several inexpensive gyms and fitness centres located near the apartment building. There is also a large park just down the street. This means that residents who want to stay fit have a number of nearby options. In contrast, there are very few other places that people could reserve to hold meetings in the neighborhood, and all of them are very costly. For example, last month I reserved a small meeting room at the library and it cost me over $200.

In the first body paragraph, the writer begins by giving reasons why Option B is not a good choice. He then contrasts these reasons with information about why Option A is a better choice. In both cases, the writer gives specific details and examples. The use of a personal story about spending $200 to reserve a room is especially effective.

Secondly, there are 250 or so people living in the apartment building. Even though having a new fitness centre in the basement would be nice, I worry that its small size could be an issue. It is only big enough for around five percent of residents to use it at one time. The function room, on the other hand, would be large enough for about one third of residents to use at the same time, and in my view that makes it a more useful improvement to the building.

In the second body paragraph, the writer repeats the organization in the first body paragraph: he begins by giving a specific, detailed reason why Option B is not a good choice. He then contrasts this with a specific, detailed reason why Option A is a better choice. Notice how the writer gives a personal example in the first body paragraph, but an example that relates to many residents of the building in this body paragraph.

So for the reasons I have outlined, I feel Option A is the better choice.

The concluding paragraph sums up the writer's opinion and explicitly states his preference.

This response has 219 words, excellent coherence and meaning, good lexical range, high readability and comprehensibility, and great task fulfillment. **Like all responses in this book, it would likely score 11 – 12.**

Practice Topic 2.3

Type out this response to a practice topic. As you type, complete the blanks in your own words. Use the response on page 57 as a guide. Then compare your completed response with the one on page 91.

Writing Task 2: Responding to Survey Questions	26 minutes

ℹ Read the following information.	**ℹ Choose the option that you prefer. Explain the reasons for your choice. Why do you prefer it? What problems are there with the other choice? Write about 150-200 words.**
Office Building Improvements You work in a large office building. The company president is planning to improve the building either by adding a cafeteria where employees could purchase healthy meals, or by adding a fitness centre where employees could work out. The president has asked all staff for their opinion.	**O Option A:** Cafeteria: It would offer a choice of meals daily, including one for vegetarians. **O Option B:** Fitness Centre: It would be free for employees between 7AM and 7 PM every day.

`1 _____` . On the whole, however, there are several reasons why Option A would be my preference.

Firstly, there are several inexpensive gyms and fitness centres located near our office building. There is also `2 _____` . This means that workers who want to stay fit have a number of nearby options. In contrast, there are very few other places nearby where people can get delicious, healthy food, and all of them are very costly. For example, yesterday I got a sandwich from a restaurant up the street from the office, but `3 _____` .

Secondly, there are 250 or so people working in this office. Even though having a new fitness centre in the building would be nice, `4 _____` . If it is not very large, only a few people will be able to use it at one time. The cafeteria, on the other hand, `5 _____` , and in my view that makes it a more useful improvement to the building.

`6 _____` , I feel Option A is the better choice.

Useful Language

These words and phrases may help you write an effective response to a Task 2 writing topic, especially one similar to the topics on this page and pages 55 and 58. There are more useful phrases on page 102.

Firstly, ...	*Use this word to give your first reason or point about something*
For example, ...	*Use this phrase to introduce an example that supports your opinion or reason about something*
in my view ...	*Use this phrase as an alternative to "in my opinion"*
— is the better choice	*Use these words when you want to say which of two options is better; note that it is incorrect to say "the best choice" if you are referring to a choice between just two options*
Secondly, ...	*Use this word to give your second reason or point about something*
There are several reasons why ...	*Use this phrase to introduce several reasons for something*

Challenge Topic 2.3

Type a response to this Writing Task 2 challenge topic in 26 minutes. Use the expert's response on page 57 as a guide. (See page 10 for a suggestion about how to get authentic practice when you type your response.) When you have finished, compare your response to the suggested response on page 92.

Writing Task 2: Responding to Survey Questions	26 minutes
❶ **Read the following information.** **Campus Improvements** You study at a small college. The college president is planning to improve the campus either by adding a new computer centre where students could use computers and print out documents, or by building a shopping area with space for a few stores. The president has asked students for their views.	❶ **Choose the option that you prefer. Explain the reasons for your choice. Why do you prefer it? What problems are there with the other choice? Write about 150-200 words.** ○ **Option A:** Computer Centre: The Centre would be free for students daily from 7 AM to 8 PM. ○ **Option B:** Shopping Area: The shops would include a bookshop, grocery store, and café.

TASK 2: TOPIC 2.4

Topic

> *Read this Writing Task 2 topic. What information in the topic is important?*
> *How could this information help you to write an effective response to the topic?*

Writing Task 2: Responding to Survey Questions	26 minutes
ℹ Read the following information. **Online or Classroom Teaching** You are a teacher at a local community college. The college administrator wants to offer online courses to students. One possibility is to offer online-only courses. The other possibility is to offer courses that combine online classes and traditional classroom learning. The administrator wants all instructors to complete an opinion survey.	**ℹ Choose the option that you prefer. Explain the reasons for your choice. Why do you prefer it? Write about 150-200 words.** O **Option A:** Online Only Courses: Students would attend all classes by logging in with their computer or mobile device. O **Option B:** Combined Online and Offline Courses: Students would have online classes plus at least one traditional class each week.

Analysis

> *Read this analysis of the topic by a test expert. Do the expert's ideas about the topic match your ideas?*

The background information describes a work situation. Although this topic focuses on a different point of view about work than some other topics, work-related questions are the most common type of Task 2 situation that you will see in CELPIP. In this case, the background information explains that an administrator at the college where you teach wants to know what teachers think about a plan to offer online courses.

The prompt asks you to choose one option, and explain why this is your choice. It specifically asks you to discuss problems with the other choice, too. If you do not do this, your score will be affected.

The first option is for the college to offer courses that are only available online. The second option is to offer courses that combine online and offline learning. Remember that neither option is better than the other, and the raters will judge your response based on the quality of your English, not based on which option you chose. A good response will give at least two clear reasons why one option is better than the other. These could be reasons that are true only for you, or reasons that are true for other teachers.

Expert's Response

Read this response by a test expert and the detailed analysis that explains why it is a good response.

Both options have some advantages, and I can see why some instructors might prefer Option A. If I had to make a choice, however, there are several reasons why I would go for Option B.

This introductory paragraph begins by suggesting that Option A has advantages. In the final sentence, the writer makes his preference clear using natural, conditional language.

For one thing, I have a lot of experience teaching traditional classes, but limited experience teaching online classes. I would like to gain more experience with the latter before I start teaching online-only classes. Courses that combine online classes with offline ones would allow me to get this experience.

In the first body paragraph, the writer gives one reason why he thinks Option B is a good choice. Because his reason is clearly related to the topic, he does not need to explain why Option A is not as good as Option B.

For another thing, although some students are comfortable learning new ideas and new subjects online, many still prefer traditional classes when they want to learn something. Courses that combine online and offline classes would allow both kinds of students to experience their preferred type of classes.

In the second body paragraph, the writer uses the same structure as in body paragraph one: he explains why he thinks Option B is a good choice using ideas and language that are clearly related to the topic.

Finally, both online and offline classes have certain benefits. Online classes are great for sharing information quickly among hundreds of students, for instance. Offline classes, in contrast, are better when teachers want students to communicate with each other. In consequence, a combined course offers a good balance of benefits.

In the third body paragraph, the writer uses a different organization. He begins by giving one benefit of online classes. He then gives a benefit of offline classes. Finally, he shows how these ideas support his choice of Option B.

So for the reasons that I have outlined, I feel Option B is the better choice.

The concluding paragraph sums up the writer's opinion and explicitly states his preference.

This response has 195 words, excellent coherence and meaning, good lexical range, high readability and comprehensibility, and great task fulfillment. **Like all responses in this book, it would likely score 11 – 12.**

Practice Topic 2.4

Type out this response to a practice topic. As you type, complete the blanks in your own words. Use the response on page 61 as a guide. Then compare your completed response with the one on page 93.

Writing Task 2: Responding to Survey Questions	26 minutes

ⓘ Read the following information.	**ⓘ Choose the option that you prefer. Explain the reasons for your choice. Why do you prefer it? What problems are there with the other choice? Write about 150-200 words.**
Online or Classroom Courses	
You are a student at a local community college. The college is planning to offer online courses. One possibility is that courses will be online only. The other possibility is that courses will combine online classes and traditional classroom learning. The college wants all students to complete an opinion survey about which option they think is better.	**O Option A:** Online Only Courses: Students would attend all classes online. They would have no traditional classes.
	O Option B: Combined Courses: Students would take traditional classes, but would also have one online class each week.

Both options have some advantages, and [1 _____]. If I had to make a choice, however, there are [2 _____].

For one thing, most instructors have a lot of experience teaching traditional classes, but less experience teaching online classes. I think they should gain more experience with the latter before teaching online-only classes. [3 _____].

For another thing, although some students, such as me, are comfortable learning new ideas and new subjects online, [4 _____]. Courses that combine online and offline classes would allow both kinds of students to experience their preference.

Finally, both online and offline classes have certain benefits. Online classes are great for sharing information quickly among hundreds of students, for instance. Offline classes, in contrast, are better [5 _____]. In consequence, a combined course offers a good balance of benefits.

[6 _____].

Useful Language

These words and phrases may help you write an effective response to a Task 2 writing topic, especially one similar to the topics on this page and pages 60 and 62. There are more useful phrases on page 102.

For the reasons that I have outlined, ...	*Use this phrase to refer back to reasons you have explained earlier in your response*
In consequence, ...	*Use this phrase to introduce a result of something.*
In contrast, ...	*Use this phrase when you want to introduce an idea or opinion that contrasts with something you have already mentioned*
many ...	*Use this word to mean "many people" in a phrase like "many believe" or "many think"; note that you can use other words in the same way, such as "some think" or "others feel" or "most believe"*
so	*Use this word to introduce a conclusion about something or to summarize your opinion when you begin your concluding paragraph*
the latter	*Use this phrase to refer back to the second of two things you have already mentioned*

Challenge Topic 2.4

Type a response to this Writing Task 2 challenge topic in 26 minutes. Use the expert's response on page 61 as a guide. (See page 10 for a suggestion about how to get authentic practice when you type your response.) When you have finished, compare your response to the suggested response on page 94.

Writing Task 2: Responding to Survey Questions	26 minutes
❶ **Read the following information.** **Online or Classroom Training** Your company is going to train all staff. One option is to do online training. The other option is to do combined training that includes online classes and traditional classes. Your manager wants your views.	❶ **Choose the option that you prefer. Explain the reasons for your choice. Why do you prefer it? What problems are there with the other choice? Write about 150-200 words.** ○ **Option A:** Online Only Training ○ **Option B:** Combined Training

TASK 2: TOPIC 2.5

Topic

> *Read this Writing Task 2 topic. What information in the topic is important?*
> *How could this information help you to write an effective response to the topic?*

Writing Task 2: Responding to Survey Questions	26 minutes
❶ **Read the following information.** **Employee Health Plan** You work for a small company that tries to be a very good place to work. The company wants to offer health insurance to employees and their families. The company has asked all employees to say which health insurance plan they would prefer, and why.	❶ **Choose the option that you prefer. Explain the reasons for your choice. Why do you prefer it? Write about 150-200 words.** ○ **Option A:** Full Plan: You would contribute 4% of your salary to this plan, which would cover 80% of the cost of prescriptions (i.e., medicines a doctor tells you to take), and 50% of other medical expenses, including dental and travel. ○ **Option B:** Limited Plan: You would contribute 1% of your salary to this plan. This plan would cover 50% of the cost of prescriptions, but it would not cover dental work, eyeglasses, travel, or any other medical expenses.

Analysis

> *Read this analysis of the topic by a test expert. Do the expert's ideas about the topic match your ideas?*

The background information describes a work situation. This is the most common type of Task 2 situation that you will see in CELPIP. In this case, the background information explains that your company wants to know which of two health insurance plans is preferable, and why.

The prompt asks you to choose one option, and explain why this is your choice. It does not specifically ask you to discuss problems with the other choice, but you can do this, if you wish. The two options are for insurance plans with different levels of benefits. Remember that neither option is better than the other, and the raters will judge your response based on the quality of your writing, not based on which option you chose. A good response will give at least two clear reasons why one option is better than the other. These could be reasons that are true only for you, or reasons that are true for other workers at the company.

Expert's Response

Read this response by a test expert and the detailed analysis that explains why it is a good response.

Both options have some advantages, and I can see why some of my co-workers might choose Option B. On the whole, however, there are several reasons why Option A would be my preference.

This introductory paragraph begins by stating that both options have advantages. In the final sentence, the writer states his preferred option using natural language.

Although the Full Plan is obviously more expensive than the Limited Plan, I think it would help most employees save money in the long term. One major benefit of the Full Plan is that it covers medical costs when travelling. As most employees take vacations each year or go on business trips, they would save money because they do not have to purchase medical travel insurance. Moreover, dental work and eyeglasses tend to be very costly, and the Full Plan pays half the cost of such expenses, meaning most employees would save money each time they visit the dentist or eye doctor. And as both insurance plans are not only for employees, but also for their families, the total savings could be significant. For instance, I calculated that the Full Plan would cost $2,000 annually but I would save $4,000 or so. In contrast, the Limited Plan would cost $500 annually but would only save me about the same amount.

In this response, the writer uses a single, long body paragraph rather than two or three shorter paragraphs. The writer begins by mentioning a disadvantage of his preferred option, but then gives three reasons why this is his choice. Notice how the writer uses clear phrases to signpost his reasons: "One major benefit …" and "Moreover, …" and finally "And as …" Also notice how the writer uses specific examples to support his reasons. Describing how much health care can cost is especially effective.

So as far as I am concerned, Option A is the better choice by far.

The concluding paragraph sums up the writer's opinion and explicitly states his preference.

This response has 208 words, excellent coherence and meaning, good lexical range, high readability and comprehensibility, and great task fulfillment. **Like all responses in this book, it would likely score 11 – 12.**

Practice Topic 2.5

Type out this response to a practice topic. As you type, complete the blanks in your own words. Use the response on page 65 as a guide. Then compare your completed response with the one on page 94.

Writing Task 2: Responding to Survey Questions	26 minutes

ℹ Read the following information.	**ℹ Choose the option that you prefer. Explain the reasons for your choice. Why do you prefer it? Write about 150-200 words.**
Employee Benefits	
You work for a small company that tries to be a very good place to work. The company wants to give all employees an additional benefit. The owner of the company has asked all employees to say which benefit they would prefer, and why.	**O Option A:** Vacation Time: Employees will get an extra two days of vacation time each year. **O Option B:** Profit Sharing: The company will share 1% of its profits with workers each year.

---

[1] .

I think that Profit Sharing would help most employees financially. One major benefit of Profit Sharing is that it encourages employees to work hard. If the company does well and makes a significant profit, [2] . Although having additional days of vacation time is attractive in some ways, [3] . Consequently, I feel that the benefits of Profit Sharing outweigh the advantages of the Vacation Time benefit.

Moreover, the Profit Sharing idea might make employees more loyal to the company. If they know that they will get a bonus each year, they are [4] . This is good for the company because hiring and training workers usually [5] . In contrast, many companies offer good vacations, so workers might not be so loyal to the company if the benefit were extra time off.

[6] .

Useful Language

These words and phrases may help you write an effective response to a Task 2 writing topic, especially one similar to the topics on this page and pages 64 and 66. There are more useful phrases on page 102.

annually	*Use this word as an alternative to words "yearly" or "each year"*
For instance, …	*Use this phrase as an alternative to "For example, …" when you want to introduce an example that supports your view about a topic*
in the long term	*Use this phrase to talk about something that will happen a fairly long time from now or that will take a long time to show an effect*
Moreover, …	*Use this word to introduce an opinion or point about something after you have already introduced a previous opinion or point*
not only … , but also …	*Use this paired phrase to introduce two related ideas; for example, you might say something like "Option A not only benefits local people, but also helps people from other countries"*
tend to	*Use this phrase to describe something that often happens or is usually true; for instance, you might say something like "people who live in cities tend to go out more often than people …"*

Challenge Topic 2.5

Type a response to this Writing Task 2 challenge topic in 26 minutes. Use the expert's response on page 65 as a guide. (See page 10 for a suggestion about how to get authentic practice when you type your response.) When you have finished, compare your response to the suggested response on page 96.

Writing Task 2: Responding to Survey Questions	**26 minutes**
❶ **Read the following information.** **Employee Benefits** You work for a large company that wants to attract excellent new employees. The company is deciding which benefit to offer new employees. Existing employees will get the same benefit, too. Your manager has asked you to say what you think.	❶ **Choose the option that you prefer. Explain the reasons for your choice. Why do you prefer it? Write about 150-200 words.** ○ **Option A:** More Vacation Time: New staff will get an extra two days of vacation each year. ○ **Option B:** Higher Salaries: New staff will get a pay rise after three months.

TASK 2: ADDITIONAL TOPICS

Use these five additional topics to get more writing practice for Task 2. You will get the most benefit if you write under test conditions. This means typing each response in 26 minutes. (The study tip on page 10 explains how to use a free online CELPIP test to get an authentic experience when typing your responses.)

Topic 2.6

| *A sample response to this topic written by a test expert is on page 96.*

Writing Task 2: Responding to Survey Questions	26 minutes
ⓘ Read the following information. **Employee Training** Your company wants all employees to become more efficient at using computers. One option is for the company to provide training at the office on Saturday mornings. The other option is for employees to visit a training centre 30 minutes away from the office on Tuesday evenings. Your manager wants to know the preference of all employees.	**ⓘ Choose the option that you prefer. Explain the reasons for your choice. Why do you prefer it? Write about 150-200 words.** **O Option A:** Training at the Office: You would have to come to the office every Saturday morning for eight weeks. Each training session would last from 9AM to 12PM. **O Option B:** Training at a Training Centre: You would have to visit the training centre every Tuesday evening for 12 weeks. Each training session would last from 6:30PM to 8:30PM.

Topic 2.7

A sample response to this topic written by a test expert is on page 98.

Writing Task 2: Responding to Survey Questions	26 minutes
ℹ Read the following information. **Company Event** Your company is planning a special lunch event in July. Your manager wants to know whether you think it would be better to have a barbeque at a local beach, or to go to a popular local restaurant that sells fresh seafood.	**ℹ Choose the option that you prefer. Explain the reasons for your choice. Why do you prefer it? Write about 150-200 words.** O **Option A:** Beach Barbeque: The company will supply all food and drinks. O **Option B:** Restaurant Lunch: The company will repay up to $50 per employee for food / drinks.

Topic 2.8

A sample response to this topic written by a test expert is on page 99.

Writing Task 2: Responding to Survey Questions	26 minutes
ℹ Read the following information. **Facilities at Work** The company you work for has a child care facility where parents can leave young children during the day. Not many people currently use the child care facility, so the company owner is thinking of replacing it with a fitness centre that would be open for all employees to use. The owner wants all workers to answer an opinion survey.	**ℹ Choose the option that you prefer. Explain the reasons for your choice. Why do you prefer it? What problems are there with the other choice? Write about 150-200 words.** O **Option A:** Fitness Centre: The company should replace the child care facility with a fitness centre. O **Option B:** Child Care Facility: The company should keep the child care facility.

Topic 2.9

A sample response to this topic written by a test expert is on page 100.

Writing Task 2: Responding to Survey Questions	26 minutes
ⓘ Read the following information. **Working from Home** Your company is planning to allow some employees to work from home for up to three days each week. Your manager wants to know whether working from home would be suitable for you or not, and why.	**ⓘ Choose the option that you prefer. Explain the reasons for your choice. Why do you prefer it? Write about 150-200 words.** **O Option A:** Work from Home: You would like to work from home up to three days each week, and you think the job you do and your home situation make working from home possible. **O Option B:** Not Working from Home: You would prefer to continue working at the office every day. You think the work you do and your home situation would make working from home hard.

Topic 2.10

A sample response to this topic written by a test expert is on page 101.

Writing Task 2: Responding to Survey Questions	26 minutes
ⓘ Read the following information. **City Development** You live in a small city. A forested area in the northern part of the city is currently undeveloped. The city council is considering two options for this area – either cutting down the forest to build a shopping centre, or turning the forest into a recreational area where people can enjoy outdoor activities. The city council wants all residents to give their opinion.	**ⓘ Choose the option that you prefer. Explain the reasons for your choice. Why do you prefer it? What problems are there with the other choice? Write about 150-200 words.** **O Option A:** Shopping Centre: The shopping centre would have around 30 stores, plus a movie theatre, and a play area for children. **O Option B:** Recreational Area: The recreational area would have trails for hiking and biking in summer and cross-country skiing in winter.

Suggestions for Finding Additional Practice Topics

Here are some suggestions for creating and finding additional writing topics for Task 2.

1. Create your own topics by making small changes to the topics in this book

It is relatively easy to come up with new topics by adapting the topics in this book (or other books). Writing Challenge 2.5 on page 67 is a good example. It changes the original topic so that instead of choosing which is the better health insurance plan, you must choose the better benefit.

In addition, because Task 2 topics in CELPIP always have two options, you can get more practice by writing two responses to each topic: one response favouring Option A, and a second response favouring Option B.

2. Borrow or purchase official CELPIP writing questions

Paragon Testing Enterprises is the organization that develops and administers the CELPIP Test. This organization sells official practice tests and study materials for CELPIP. You may be able to borrow these from the library or purchase them online from this website: `https://www.paragontesting.ca/`

3. Find unofficial CELPIP writing questions on the Internet

Unlike with Writing Task 1, there are no writing tasks in other tests like IELTS that are similar to Writing Task 2 in CELPIP. However, if you search the Internet for "CELPIP writing topics" or similar, you may find some questions that you can use for additional writing practice.

Note: Be careful with topics you find online. Some of them may be close to the real questions you will see in the CELPIP Test, but some of them may not be similar. If you worry that a question you found online is not a good question, it may be better not to use that question.

SUGGESTED RESPONSES

Response to Practice Topic 1.1

> *Check your answers to the practice topic on page 20. If you are not sure why an answer is correct (or incorrect), consult a dictionary, look in a grammar book, search the Internet, or ask a teacher.*

Writing Task 1: Writing an Email	27 minutes

ℹ **Read the following information.**	ℹ **In about 150-200 words, write an email to the city council. Your email should do the following things:**
You live near a park. Recently, some students from a local college have been spending time in the park in the evenings and at night. They talk loudly, play noisy games, and listen to loud music.	• Give information about where you live. • Describe the problem and how it affects you. • Say what you would like the city council to do about the problem.

Dear Sir or Madam

I live 1 **at** 123 New Street in Newtown, Manitoba. My home is just across the street from the entrance 2 **to** North Lake Park.

I am writing to complain about noise 3 **from / in** the park. Since last month, some students from Newtown College have been hanging out in the park from approximately 8PM 4 **to / until** very late. They do this most days, but especially 5 **at / on** weekends. The students talk and play music loudly, and sometimes they even play soccer or other sports and games. This has a big impact on my life because the noise makes it hard 6 **for** me and my family to sleep.

I would like you to put up signs in North Lake Park asking people to be quiet if they use the park in the evening or 7 **at** night. Alternatively, I would like you to lock the park 8 **at / after** 8PM so that nobody can hang out there after dark and disturb others 9 **by** being noisy. I am sure that other people living on my street would feel happier if you adopted one 10 **of** these suggestions.

Thank you,

Mr R Smith

189 words

Response to Challenge Topic 1.1

Compare your response to the challenge topic on page 21 with the one written by a test expert below.
As with every response in this book, the expert's response would probably get a score of 11 – 12.

Writing Task 1: Writing an Email	27 minutes

 **Read the following information.**	 **In about 150-200 words, write an email to the owner of the nightclub. Your email should do the following things:**
A popular new nightclub has opened near where you live. The noise from the nightclub is very loud, and many people who visit the club are also noisy when they arrive and leave.	• Give information about where you live. • Describe the problem and say how it affects you. • Say how you think the owner could resolve the issue.

Dear Nightclub Owner

I live at 123 New Street in Newtown, Manitoba. My home is just across the street from the nightclub that you own at 128 New Street.

I am writing to complain about noise from the club. Since the club opened, I have been disturbed by noise from the club and from your customers. The music, which starts at 7PM and ends after 3AM is very loud, and people going to the club laugh and shout as they arrive and leave, and this has a big impact on my life. The noise makes it impossible for me or my family to sleep properly.

I would like you to play music at your club more quietly and to add some kind of barrier to block the noise. I would also like you to ask your customers to think about local people when they arrive and leave. This would not be perfect for me, as I am sure that I would still hear some noise, but it would definitely improve the situation. I am sure that other people living on my street would feel happier if you adopted these ideas.

Thank you,

Mr R Smith

194 words

Response to Practice Topic 1.2

> Check your answers to the practice topic on page 24. If you are not sure why an answer is correct (or incorrect), consult a dictionary, look in a grammar book, search the Internet, or ask a teacher.

Writing Task 1: Writing an Email	27 minutes

ℹ Read the following information.	**ℹ In about 150-200 words, write an email to your employee. Your email should do the following things:**
You are a manager at a company. One of your employees has excellent ideas and works hard. However, this person is thinking about quitting work in order to go back to university.	• Say why you think this person is a good worker. • Describe some of the disadvantages of quitting work to attend university. • Mention some benefits of continuing to work at the company.

Dear Mary

I have heard that you are considering quitting your job at this company in order to attend university. I **1 have been** impressed with your ideas and with how hard you work. In my view you are an excellent employee, and it **2 is** my hope that you will reconsider your plan.

I see several issues with quitting your job. As you **3 know**, the economy is not doing well at the moment and few companies **4 are** hiring new workers. I have read many reports that **5 say** this situation will probably continue for a number of years. When you look for work again after going back to university, I am worried that you may find it hard to get a job.

Although many employers want to hire those who have a university education, they **6 are** often more interested in employing people with relevant work experience. As a result, continuing to work in this job **7 will give** you valuable work skills. With improved skills you may get a promotion at this company, or you may find a great position at another company. For these two reasons, I strongly advise you to continue working.

Please come to my office anytime if you **8 wish** to discuss this further.

Robert Smith

206 words

Response to Challenge Topic 1.2

Compare your response to the challenge topic on page 25 with the one written by a test expert below. As with every response in this book, the expert's response would probably get a score of 11 – 12.

Writing Task 1: Writing an Email	27 minutes

ℹ **Read the following information.**	ℹ **In about 150-200 words, write an email to your friend. Your email should do the following things:**
Your friend is an excellent cook. For many years, your friend has wanted to become a chef. Recently, however, your friend is thinking of giving up this dream and getting a job working in a store.	• Say why you think your friend is good at cooking. • Describe some of the benefits to your friend of trying to achieve his or her dream. • Mention some disadvantages of finding a job working in a store.

Dear Mary

I have heard that you are considering giving up your dream of becoming a chef in order to get a job at a store. I think you are an amazing cook. The meal you prepared last week was the most delicious food I have ever eaten. I really hope that you will reconsider your plan.

If you try to achieve your dream, I think you will be much happier than if you give up your dream. As you know, I gave up my dream of becoming a lawyer, and I think that this was a mistake. Even if you don't succeed, you will know that you tried your best. If you give up now, I think you will always regret it.

I see two main problems with getting a job in a store. First, the economy is not doing well at the moment and few companies are hiring. So you may not find work easily. And second, most jobs in stores do not pay well. I am worried that you will have money problems if you choose to get a job in the retail industry.

Give me a call if you want to talk about this.

Robert

199 words

Response to Practice Topic 1.3

> Check your answers to the practice topic on page 28. If you are not sure why an answer is correct (or incorrect), consult a dictionary, look in a grammar book, search the Internet, or ask a teacher. Note that the symbol Ø means no article is needed.

Writing Task 1: Writing an Email	27 minutes
ℹ Read the following information. Every year you and several old friends spend a few days together in the winter. This year, your friend Sam is organizing things. You want to suggest an activity that you think everyone would enjoy.	**ℹ In about 150-200 words, write an email to your friend. Your email should do the following things:** • Describe the activity you think you and your friends should do this year. • Give details about where the activity is and how much it costs. • Explain why this activity is good for everyone.

Hi Mary

I hope you and your family are well. Things here are fine.

As you know, our old friends' day is coming soon. I have **1 an** idea for something we could do that I think we'd all enjoy. How about going skiing for **2 the / a** day?

Blue Mountain is **3 a** resort north of Toronto that has some good places to ski. It's easy to get there by car or bus. I went there last year with my family, and it took only two hours or so. There are **4 a** lot of hotels around there that are relatively inexpensive, and **5 the / Ø** ski tickets are pretty cheap, too.

There are several reasons why I think this would be great. First, everyone in our group loves skiing, especially when Bob falls over! And **6 Ø** Blue Mountain has some great shops, restaurants, and nightclubs, too, so we can also enjoy **7 the / Ø** evenings and other times when we're not skiing.

Give me **8 a** call so we can discuss further.

Robert

168 words

Response to Challenge Topic 1.3

Compare your response to the challenge topic on page 29 with the one written by a test expert below.
As with every response in this book, the expert's response would probably get a score of 11 – 12.

Writing Task 1: Writing an Email	27 minutes

 **Read the following information.**

Every year your company arranges a fun event for all employees. This year, one of your colleagues is in charge of organizing the event. You want to suggest an activity that you think everyone in the company would enjoy.

 **In about 150-200 words, write an email to your colleague. Your email should do the following things:**

- Describe the activity you recommend.
- Give details about what the activity is.
- Explain why this activity is good for everyone in the company.

Dear Mary

I understand that you are in charge of organizing the company event day this year. I have an idea for something we could do that I think everyone would enjoy. Have you considered going to a museum?

The National Science museum has just opened on North Lake Street. It's about 20 minutes by bus or car from the office. I went to the museum with my family about a week ago. We all had a great time. You can read many positive reviews of the museum online, too.

There are several reasons why I think this would be great. First, the museum has an exhibit about the history of computers at the moment. As our company makes computers, I think this would be very interesting for people to see. Second, the museum has a great restaurant that serves delicious food, so we could all have a nice lunch. And third, because the museum has just opened, tickets are half price right now, so it would not cost the company a lot of money.

Drop by my office if you want more details or to discuss further.

Robert

189 words

Response to Practice Topic 1.4

> *Check your answers to the practice topic on page 32. If you are not sure why an answer is correct (or incorrect), consult a dictionary, look in a grammar book, search the Internet, or ask a teacher.*

Writing Task 1: Writing an Email	27 minutes

ℹ️ Read the following information.	**ℹ️ In about 150-200 words, write an email to your friend. Your email should do the following things:**
You recently saw a police officer prevent a woman from being hit by a car. Your friend has asked you to describe what you saw.	• Explain where you saw the police officer help the woman. • Give details about how and why the woman almost got hit by a car. • Describe how the police officer helped the woman and what happened afterwards.

Hi Mary

I hope you and your family are well. Things here are fine. As you requested, **I am writing** to tell you about a situation I saw **the other day**.

I was walking home **two days ago** along the North River near Newtown. I had just passed the Old Bridge **when I saw** a woman jogging. She was **listening to loud music** and wearing **dark sunglasses**.

As I watched her, she suddenly turned and started to run across the road. A truck was driving towards her **very quickly,** and the driver used his horn to warn her. However, **because** she was wearing sunglasses and headphones, I think the woman did not see or hear him.

Suddenly, I saw a police officer run towards the woman. She pushed the woman out of the way of the truck and then jumped out of the way herself. The jogging woman fell over, but she was not hurt by the fall or by **the truck**. She thanked the police officer **many times** for saving her life.

Give me a call if you any questions about what I saw.

Robert

186 words

Test Expert Writing Practice *for* CELPIP®

Response to Challenge Topic 1.4

Compare your response to the challenge topic on page 33 with the one written by a test expert below.
As with every response in this book, the expert's response would probably get a score of 11 – 12.

Writing Task 1: Writing an Email	27 minutes

 **Read the following information.**

You recently went on a business trip. During your trip, you saw a demonstration of a new computer. Your boss thinks the computer might be useful for your company. Your boss wants you to describe what you saw.

In about 150-200 words, write an email to your boss. Your email should do the following things:

- Explain where you saw the demonstration.
- Give details about what the computer is like and what it can do.
- Say whether you think the computer would be useful for your company, and why.

Dear Ms Jones

As you requested, I am writing to tell you about the computer demonstration I saw during my recent business trip to Europe.

I attended a conference in London. While I was at the conference, I noticed that a company called New Tech was selling a new type of computer. I spoke to one of the people working for New Tech, and he kindly gave me a demonstration of the computer.

The computer is very fast. It starts up in less than 12 seconds, and can open any program in two seconds or less. It has a very large screen, which is clear and easy to see, and you can control the computer by touching the screen as well as by using a mouse and keyboard. Finally, the computer has a lot of useful software installed on it, including Office.

In my view, New Tech computers would be good for the company. In addition to the benefits I just mentioned, they are inexpensive – they cost less than $1000 each – and if a computer stops working in the first three years, New Tech will fix it for free.

Let me know if you would like more information about these computers.

Robert Smith

203 words

Response to Practice Topic 1.5

> *Check your answers to the practice topic on page 36. If you are not sure why an answer is correct (or incorrect), consult a dictionary, look in a grammar book, search the Internet, or ask a teacher.*

Writing Task 1: Writing an Email	27 minutes

ℹ **Read the following information.**	ℹ **In about 150-200 words, write an email to the cruise ship company. Your email should do the following things:**
You recently took a short cruise vacation with your family. The staff on the ship were excellent and took very good care of you. It was the best vacation you have ever taken.	• Explain when you went on the cruise, for how long, and where. • Give some examples of the service you received. • State how you feel about the ship and its staff.

Dear Sir or Madam

Last month my family and I took a five-night cruise vacation with your company. We travelled in Europe from Norway south to the United Kingdom. We are **1 so / very** happy about our decision to take a vacation with your company because we received great service and had a wonderful time.

When we arrived in Norway, a young woman from your staff was at the airport to greet us. Our hotel lost our reservation, but she helped us sort the problem out **2 effectively / quickly** and easily. Next day she drove us and several other families to the cruise ship. While we were enjoying the cruise, the great service continued from **3 almost / nearly** every member of staff. In addition, we were **4 incredibly / really** happy with the wonderful food and the excellent activities and entertainment. All in all, it was **5 truly** a fantastic trip.

I can **6 honestly** say that your staff provided wonderful service, and I would like to thank you and everybody who works on your cruise ship. Everyone in my family wants to take another cruise with your company next year, and I will definitely recommend you to my friends and colleagues, too.

Yours

Mr Robert Smith

200 words

Response to Challenge Topic 1.5

Compare your response to the challenge topic on page 37 with the one written by a test expert below. As with every response in this book, the expert's response would probably get a score of 11 – 12.

Writing Task 1: Writing an Email	27 minutes

ℹ Read the following information.

You recently stayed at a hotel for a few nights. The staff at the hotel were unprofessional and did not provide you with good care. It was the worst service you have ever received at a hotel.

ℹ In about 150-200 words, write an email to the hotel manager. Your email should do the following things:

- Explain when you stayed at the hotel, for how long, and why.
- Give some examples of the service you received.
- State how you feel about the hotel and its staff.

Dear Sir or Madam

Last week I had to go to Boston on business. After reading some reviews online, I decided to stay at your hotel from Monday to Wednesday night. I regret my decision because I received such terrible service.

When I arrived on Monday evening, I was late and hungry because of a delayed flight. Despite my hunger, the young woman working at the front desk told me the kitchen was closed and refused to help me find a restaurant that was open. She just told me "Walk around. Maybe you'll find one." In addition, when I left the hotel on Thursday morning, I realized that I had left several items in my room. I asked a different young woman if I could go back to my room to collect them, but she said "No" and told me that if I wanted the hotel to send the items to me, I would have to pay.

I am sad to say that your staff provided some of the worst service I have ever experienced in my life. I will definitely never stay at your hotel again. Not only that, but I will recommend that my friends and colleagues avoid your hotel, too.

Yours

Mr Robert Smith

207 words

Response to Additional Topic 1.6

Compare your response to Additional Topic 1.6 on page 38 with the one written by a test expert below. As with every response in this book, the expert's response would probably get a score of 11 – 12.

Writing Task 1: Writing an Email	27 minutes

ⓘ Read the following information.	**ⓘ In about 150-200 words, write an email to a local company. Your email should do the following things:**
You volunteer at a local hospital for children. Your manager has asked you to contact local businesses to raise money for new equipment to save children's lives.	• Explain who you are and why you are writing. • Describe how the hospital will use any money that is raised. • Say how much money you need and how the company can donate it

Hello

I am volunteering at Newtown Children's Hospital in Newtown, Manitoba. The hospital is trying to raise money to buy new equipment. I am hoping that your business would be willing to donate some money to help us achieve this important goal.

The Children's Hospital wants to help children who have problems with their heart. To do this, we need some expensive new equipment. Every dollar that is donated by generous companies like yours will be used to buy equipment that doctors say could save many children with serious heart disease.

The hospital's goal is to raise $100,000 before the end of next year. We would be happy to accept any amount that your company can give. If you can give a donation, as a thank you, the hospital will mention your company in our annual newsletter. To donate, please call me on 1 888 123 4567 (extension 45), send me an email at this address, or visit the hospital's website.

Thank you in advance.

Robert Smith

167 words

Response to Additional Topic 1.7

Compare your response to Additional Topic 1.7 on page 38 with the one written by a test expert below. As with every response in this book, the expert's response would probably get a score of 11 – 12.

Writing Task 1: Writing an Email	27 minutes

Read the following information.	**ⓘ** **In about 150-200 words, write an email to your co-workers. Your email should do the following things:**
Every day you take lunch to work and leave it in a refrigerator at your office. For the last few days, somebody has been eating part of your lunch.	• Explain why you bring lunch every day and what your lunch looks like. • Say what has been happening for the last few days and how it makes you feel. • Describe what you will do if somebody continues to eat items of food from your lunch.

Hi Everyone

I bring lunch to the office every day because I have health problems and I need to eat special foods that are difficult to find and costly to buy at the shops near the office. I always put my food in the office fridge in a blue plastic box.

Unfortunately, recently somebody has begun eating some of my lunch each day. This makes me feel very sad, because somebody is choosing to take my food rather than buy or prepare their own. I am also hungry, of course, because I do not eat a full lunch each day. Finally, if I cannot eat the special food I need, I may get sick.

So, I would like to ask the person who is taking my lunch to stop, please. I hope that this email is enough. If somebody continues taking food from my blue plastic lunch box, I will ask our manager to help me find the person who is responsible.

Thanks,

Robert (in the accounts department)

168 words

Response to Additional Topic 1.8

Compare your response to Additional Topic 1.8 on page 39 with the one written by a test expert below. As with every response in this book, the expert's response would probably get a score of 11 – 12.

Writing Task 1: Writing an Email	27 minutes

ⓘ Read the following information.	**ⓘ In about 150-200 words, write an email to the manager of the restaurant. Your email should do the following things:**
You recently went out for dinner at a popular and expensive restaurant near your home. It was not a good experience: the service was average, the food was poor, and you were charged too much. Neither the chef nor the restaurant manager was available to help you.	• Explain when you went to the restaurant, why, and what you expected. • Give examples of the problems you experienced while eating there. • Suggest how the manager could fix the issues to your satisfaction.

Dear Sir or Madam

Last week my wife and I had our 25th wedding anniversary. We decided to go out for a special meal, and we chose your restaurant because it is popular and has a great reputation. We were expecting to have delicious food and a wonderful experience. Unfortunately, we had a terrible time and neither the chef nor the manager was available to solve our problems.

For one thing, even though we reserved a table, we had to wait for 90 minutes before we could sit down. For another thing, our waiter twice got our orders wrong, frequently failed to bring things that we had ordered, and gave us pressure to order expensive drinks that we did not want. Finally, although the food tasted good, most of it was cold by the time we got it.

My wife and I would still like to celebrate our anniversary at a special place. To say sorry for the poor experience we had last week, would you be willing to give us a discount worth 50% off the price of a meal for two?

I look forward to a positive response.

Mr R Smith

193 words

Response to Additional Topic 1.9

Compare your response to Additional Topic 1.9 on page 39 with the one written by a test expert below. As with every response in this book, the expert's response would probably get a score of 11 – 12.

Writing Task 1: Writing an Email	27 minutes

ℹ **Read the following information.**	ℹ **In about 150-200 words, write an email to the person organizing the hiking group. Your email should do the following things:**
You saw a poster at the library about a new hiking group that is starting in your area. You love hiking and would like to join this group.	<ul><li>Say who you are and why you would like to join the hiking group.</li><li>Ask how you can become a member and how often the group will meet.</li><li>Suggest some places you have previously been that are good for hiking.</li></ul>

Hi

My name is Robert. I was at the public library the other day and I saw a poster advertising the new hiking group that you are starting. I've loved hiking since I was a child, and I would like to join your group, if it's still possible.

Please could you send me some more information about the group? I would especially like to know the following information:

1. How can I become a member, and is there a membership fee?
2. How often will the group meet to go hiking?
3. Where are some of the places you will go hiking?

Since I moved to Newtown last year, I've hiked in a number of beautiful areas. I can especially recommend the Old Forest, the path along the North River, and the area around Glass Lake. Of course, I would love to go hiking in some new areas of the countryside, too!

I hope to hear from you soon.

Robert Smith

161 words

Response to Additional Topic 1.10

Compare your response to Additional Topic 1.10 on page 40 with the one written by a test expert below. As with every response in this book, the expert's response would probably get a score of 11 – 12.

Writing Task 1: Writing an Email	27 minutes

ℹ Read the following information.	**ℹ In about 150-200 words, write an email to the store manager. Your email should do the following things:**
You recently shopped at a store that is two hours from your home by car. When you got home, you realized that the store charged you too much. You called the store, but were told you had to return in person to have the extra charge corrected.	• Say which items you purchased and were overcharged for. • Explain why you do not wish to return to the store in person. • Suggest what actions the manager could take to solve the problem.

Dear Sir or Madam

Two days ago I drove out to your store. It took me two hours by car, but I wanted to buy some items that were on sale. In particular, I purchased a sleeping bag and a large tent. These items were supposed to be on sale for 50% off, but when I got home, I saw that my discount was only 25%.

I called your store to ask somebody to refund the extra cost. Unfortunately, I was told that I would have to drive back to the store so the manager could refund my money in person. This would take me more than four hours – two hours there and two hours back plus time in the store – and I am busy so I cannot spend that much time. It would also cost me a lot to pay for the gas to drive there.

Please find a way to refund the extra charge by telephone or online so that I do not have to return to the store in person.

I look forward to hearing from you.

Mr R Smith

183 words

Response to Practice Topic 2.1

Compare your response to the practice topic on page 50 with the one written by a test expert below.

As with every response in this book, the expert's response would probably get a score of 11 – 12.

Writing Task 2: Responding to Survey Questions	26 minutes

ℹ **Read the following information.**	ℹ **Choose the option that you prefer. Explain the reasons for your choice. Why do you prefer your choice? Write about 150-200 words.**
Transportation to Training Session	
Your company is holding a special training session for all senior employees next week. The training will take place at a location about one hour away from the office. The person organizing the training wants your opinion about the best way for staff to travel to the training location.	O **Option A:** Individual Transportation: Workers should use their own transportation to travel to the training session.
	O **Option B:** Group Transportation: The company should arrange transportation to take staff to the training session.

Both options have some advantages, and I can see why some of my colleagues might choose Option A. On the whole, however, there are several reasons why Option B would be my preference.

For one thing, if the company were to arrange transportation, everybody would arrive on time and nobody would get lost. At past training sessions, some people who travelled on their own have been late. This caused the people who arrived on time to become frustrated while waiting for them.

For another thing, if people know they do not have to drive themselves, they can relax and focus on the training more. In contrast, people travelling to the training session in their own cars might not be able to concentrate because of concern about driving home in heavy traffic after it finished.

Finally, if the company arranges transportation for everyone, people can chat with each other on the way to and from the session. This will promote good feelings and allow people to discuss what they learned during the training. If a lot of people were travelling to the training on their own, however, this would not be possible.

So as far as I am concerned, Option B is the better choice.

204 words

Response to Challenge Topic 2.1

> *Compare your response to the challenge topic on page 51 with the one written by a test expert below. As with every response in this book, the expert's response would probably get a score of 11 – 12.*

Writing Task 2: Responding to Survey Questions	26 minutes

ℹ Read the following information.	**ℹ Choose the option that you prefer. Explain the reasons for your choice. Why do you prefer your choice? Write about 150-200 words.**
Transportation to Meeting Your company is holding a meeting for many staff members next month. The meeting will take place in another city. The person organizing the meeting wants to know whether employees prefer to travel to this city by train or by bus.	**O Option A:** Train: The journey takes five hours. Employees arrive in the other city at 9 PM. **O Option B:** Bus: The journey takes nine hours. Employees travel overnight and arrive in the other city at 6 AM.

Both options have some advantages, and I can see why some of my colleagues might choose Option B. On the whole, however, there are several reasons why Option A would be my preference.

For one thing, if the company were to arrange transportation by bus, many employees might find it hard to sleep on the bus at night. This would mean that people would be tired the next day, and might not be able to concentrate during the meeting. In contrast, if employees take the train to the other city, they would arrive in time to spend the night in a hotel and they would all probably sleep better.

For another thing, I know that a lot of people, including myself, feel sick when they travel by bus. I am worried that if the company were to arrange bus transportation, some employees would be sick. Again, this might affect their ability to concentrate during the meeting the next day. On the other hand, I think most people can travel by train without feeling sick.

So as far as I am concerned, Option A is the better choice.

187 words

Response to Practice Topic 2.2

Compare your response to the practice topic on page 54 with the one written by a test expert below. As with every response in this book, the expert's response would probably get a score of 11 – 12.

Writing Task 2: Responding to Survey Questions	26 minutes

ⓘ Read the following information.

Reward for Employees

Your company has been successful recently, and your manager wants to reward everyone. One option is to hold a large party for all employees. The second option is to give all employees one extra day off. Your manager wants to know what you think.

ⓘ Choose the option that you prefer. Explain the reasons for your choice. Why do you prefer it? What problems are there with the other choice? Write about 150-200 words.

O **Option A:** Party for Employees: The party would be held on a Saturday or Sunday.

O **Option B:** Extra Day Off: Employees would have to use the extra day off within six weeks.

Both options have some advantages, and I can see why some of my co-workers might prefer Option A. If I had to make a choice, however, there are several reasons why I would go for Option B.

On the one hand, a party would be fun and a nice way to celebrate the company's success. However, the company already hosts a summer picnic, which is coming up soon, and having two events for staff so close together seems unnecessary. And because the party would be held on a Saturday or Sunday, some people might already have plans and would be unable to attend.

On the other hand, if employees were to get an extra day off, all of them would benefit depending on their needs or wishes. I expect some would choose to spend the day doing regular things like shopping or doing work around the home. Others might combine the extra day with some vacation days and take a short trip somewhere nice. And still others might use the day just to relax and enjoy the beautiful summer weather. In other words, an extra day off would give employees more choice.

So for the reasons that I have outlined, I feel Option B is the better choice.

208 words

Response to Challenge Topic 2.2

Compare your response to the challenge topic on page 55 with the one written by a test expert below. As with every response in this book, the expert's response would probably get a score of 11 – 12.

Writing Task 2: Responding to Survey Questions	26 minutes

ⓘ Read the following information.	**ⓘ** Choose the option that you prefer. Explain the reasons for your choice. Why do you prefer it? What problems are there with the other choice? Write about 150-200 words.
Financial Bonus from Your City	
The city where you live recently received a large sum of money from the government. The city council will use the money to benefit local people. One option is to give every resident, excluding children, a small sum of money. The other option is to give taxpayers a tax rebate.	O **Option A:** Money: Each adult resident of the city would get $500 immediately.
	O **Option B:** Tax Rebate: All taxpayers would get a rebate worth up to $600 at the end of the year.

Both options have some advantages, and I can see why some local people might prefer Option B. If I had to make a choice, however, there are several reasons why I would go for Option A.

Firstly, although it would be nice to get $600 instead of $500, this money is not guaranteed. The information says that the rebate is worth "up to $600." This means that the amount residents receive could be less than $600. And in fact, it could even be less than $500.

Secondly, I believe that most people, including myself, would prefer to have money now than to wait until the end of the year. Even people who do not have anything they need to purchase right now could invest the money and make some money from their investments.

Finally, many people have a lot of expenses at the end of the year, so the tax rebate would be used up to pay for things like holiday gifts, or end-of-year events. In contrast, I think that few people have major expenses right now, so the sum of money would feel like a nice bonus.

So for the reasons that I have outlined, I feel Option A is the better choice.

204 words

Response to Practice Topic 2.3

> *Compare your response to the practice topic on page 58 with the one written by a test expert below.
> As with every response in this book, the expert's response would probably get a score of 11 – 12.*

Writing Task 2: Responding to Survey Questions	26 minutes

ⓘ Read the following information.

Office Building Improvements

You work in a large office building. The company president is planning to improve the building either by adding a cafeteria where employees could purchase healthy meals, or by adding a fitness centre where employees could work out. The president has asked all staff for their opinion.

ⓘ Choose the option that you prefer. Explain the reasons for your choice. Why do you prefer it? What problems are there with the other choice? Write about 150-200 words.

O **Option A:** Cafeteria: It would offer a choice of meals daily, including one for vegetarians.

O **Option B:** Fitness Centre: It would be free for employees between 7ᴀᴍ and 7 ᴘᴍ every day.

Both options have some advantages, and I can see why some of my co-workers might choose Option B. On the whole, however, there are several reasons why Option A would be my preference.

Firstly, there are several inexpensive gyms and fitness centres located near our office building. There is also a large park just down the street. This means that workers who want to stay fit have a number of nearby options. In contrast, there are very few other places nearby where people can get delicious, healthy food, and all of them are very costly. For example, yesterday I got a sandwich from a restaurant up the street from the office, but it cost me over $15.

Secondly, there are 250 or so people working in this office. Even though having a new fitness centre in the building would be nice, I worry that its size could be an issue. If it is not very large, only a few people will be able to use it at one time. The cafeteria, on the other hand, would probably be large enough for many staff to use at the same time, and in my view that makes it a more useful improvement to the building.

So for the reasons I have outlined, I feel Option A is the better choice.

218 words

Response to Challenge Topic 2.3

> *Compare your response to the challenge topic on page 59 with the one written by a test expert below.*
> *As with every response in this book, the expert's response would probably get a score of 11 – 12.*

Writing Task 2: Responding to Survey Questions	26 minutes

 Read the following information.

Campus Improvements

You study at a small college. The college president is planning to improve the campus either by adding a new computer centre where students could use computers and print out documents, or by building a shopping area with space for a few stores. The president has asked students for their views.

 Choose the option that you prefer. Explain the reasons for your choice. Why do you prefer it? What problems are there with the other choice? Write about 150-200 words.

O **Option A:** Computer Centre: The Centre would be free for students daily from 7 AM to 8 PM.

O **Option B:** Shopping Area: The shops would include a bookshop, grocery store, and café.

Both options have some advantages, and I can see why some students at the college might choose Option A. On the whole, however, there are several reasons why Option B would be my preference.

In terms of Option A, I think that the vast majority of students already have their own computer. Many of them also have their own printer, too, and the college library has many printers for students to use. This means that there is limited need for the computer centre, in my view. My feeling is that building it would not improve the campus at all.

In contrast, the campus does not have many shops right now, so a new shopping area would be very beneficial. The new bookshop would be a great option because currently the closest bookshop is in the centre of town, which is not very convenient. Moreover, the only place to buy food on campus right now is a convenience store. It does not sell healthy food options, so a grocery store and café would be great additions to the campus, in my view.

So for the reasons I have outlined, I feel Option B is the better choice.

196 words

Response to Practice Topic 2.4

Compare your response to the practice topic on page 62 with the one written by a test expert below. As with every response in this book, the expert's response would probably get a score of 11 – 12.

Writing Task 2: Responding to Survey Questions	26 minutes

ⓘ Read the following information.

Online or Classroom Courses

You are a student at a local community college. The college is planning to offer online courses. One possibility is that courses will be online only. The other possibility is that courses will combine online classes and traditional classroom learning. The college wants all students to complete an opinion survey about which option they think is better.

ⓘ Choose the option that you prefer. Explain the reasons for your choice. Why do you prefer it? What problems are there with the other choice? Write about 150-200 words.

O **Option A:** Online Only Courses: Students would attend all classes online. They would have no traditional classes.

O **Option B:** Combined Courses: Students would take traditional classes, but would also have one online class each week.

Both options have some advantages, and I can see why some students at the college might prefer Option A. If I had to make a choice, however, there are several reasons why I would go for Option B.

For one thing, most instructors have a lot of experience teaching traditional classes, but less experience teaching online classes. I think they should gain more experience with the latter before teaching online-only classes. Courses that combine online and offline classes would let them get this experience.

For another thing, although some students, such as me, are comfortable learning new ideas and new subjects online, many still prefer traditional classes when they want to learn something. Courses that combine online and offline classes would allow both kinds of students to experience their preference.

Finally, both online and offline classes have certain benefits. Online classes are great for sharing information quickly among hundreds of students, for instance. Offline classes, in contrast, are better when teachers want students to communicate with each other. In consequence, a combined course offers a good balance of benefits.

So for the reasons that I have outlined, I feel Option B is the better choice.

195 words

Response to Challenge Topic 2.4

> *Compare your response to the challenge topic on page 63 with the one written by a test expert below. As with every response in this book, the expert's response would probably get a score of 11 – 12.*

Writing Task 2: Responding to Survey Questions	26 minutes
ℹ️ **Read the following information.** **Online or Classroom Training** Your company is going to train all staff. One option is to do online training. The other option is to do combined training that includes online classes and traditional classes. Your manager wants your views.	ℹ️ **Choose the option that you prefer. Explain the reasons for your choice. Why do you prefer it? What problems are there with the other choice? Write about 150-200 words.** O **Option A:** Online Only Training O **Option B:** Combined Training

Both options have some advantages, and I can see why some staff members might prefer Option B. If I had to make a choice, however, there are several reasons why I would go for Option A.

For one thing, we can do the online training whenever we have time. For instance, if I have a heavy schedule one week, but a light schedule the next week, I can delay the training until my schedule is not so busy. This would not be possible with the combined training, because traditional classes have to take place at a set time.

For another thing, we can do the online training from wherever we are. For example, if I have a laptop computer, I can take part in the online training at work, at home, in a hotel, or even while travelling to a business meeting in another city. Again, this would not be possible with the combined training, because traditional classes have to take place at a set location.

So for the reasons that I have outlined, I feel Option A is the better choice.

182 words

Response to Practice Topic 2.5

> *Compare your response to the practice topic on page 66 with the one written by a test expert below.*
> *As with every response in this book, the expert's response would probably get a score of 11 – 12.*

Writing Task 2: Responding to Survey Questions	26 minutes

ℹ️ **Read the following information.**	ℹ️ **Choose the option that you prefer. Explain the reasons for your choice. Why do you prefer it? What problems are there with the other choice? Write about 150-200 words.**
Employee Benefits You work for a small company that tries to be a very good place to work. The company wants to give all employees an additional benefit. The owner of the company has asked all employees to say which benefit they would prefer, and why.	O **Option A:** Vacation Time: Employees will get an extra two days of vacation time each year. O **Option B:** Profit Sharing: The company will share 1% of its profits with workers each year.

Both options have some advantages, and I can see why some employees might choose Option A. On the whole, however, there are several reasons why Option B would be my preference.

I think that Profit Sharing would help most employees financially. One major benefit of Profit Sharing is that it encourages employees to work hard. If the company does well and makes a significant profit, everyone will get a nice financial bonus each year. Although having additional days of vacation time is attractive in some ways, going on vacation can be expensive. Consequently, I feel that the benefits of Profit Sharing outweigh the advantages of the Vacation Time benefit.

Moreover, the Profit Sharing idea might make employees more loyal to the company. If they know that they will get a bonus each year, they are less likely to look for work at another company. This is good for the company because hiring and training workers usually costs a lot of money and takes a lot of time. In contrast, many companies offer good vacations, so workers might not be so loyal to the company if the benefit were extra time off.

So as far as I am concerned, Option B is the better choice by far.

206 words

Response to Challenge Topic 2.5

> *Compare your response to the challenge topic on page 67 with the one written by a test expert below. As with every response in this book, the expert's response would probably get a score of 11 – 12.*

Writing Task 2: Responding to Survey Questions	26 minutes

ⓘ Read the following information.	**ⓘ Choose the option that you prefer. Explain the reasons for your choice. Why do you prefer it? Write about 150-200 words.**
Employee Benefits	
You work for a large company that wants to attract excellent new employees. The company is deciding which benefit to offer new employees. Existing employees will get the same benefit, too. Your manager has asked you to say what you think.	**O Option A:** More Vacation Time: New staff will get an extra two days of vacation each year. **O Option B:** Higher Salaries: New staff will get a pay rise after three months.

Both options have some advantages, and I can see why some people might choose Option A. On the whole, however, there are several reasons why Option B would be my preference.

I think that higher salaries are far more important these days than vacation time. I read an interesting article in a newspaper the other day. According to what I read, the cost of living has increased every year for the past ten years. This means that it is becoming more expensive to rent a home, buy groceries and other essential items, and even pay bills. To give an example, five years ago, my household expenses were $1,500 per month or so. Last year, however, I paid an average of approximately $1,800 per month. Having more vacation time would not help people deal with the higher cost of living, but having a higher salary would be attractive to new employees and beneficial to current employees, as well.

So as far as I am concerned, Option B is the better choice by far.

172 words

Response to Additional Topic 2.6

> *Compare your response to Additional Topic 2.6 on page 68 with the one written by a test expert below. As with every response in this book, the expert's response would probably get a score of 11 – 12.*

Writing Task 2: Responding to Survey Questions	26 minutes

ℹ Read the following information.

Employee Training

Your company wants all employees to become more efficient at using computers. One option is for the company to provide training at the office on Saturday mornings. The other option is for employees to visit a training centre 30 minutes away from the office on Tuesday evenings. Your manager wants to know the preference of all employees.

ℹ Choose the option that you prefer. Explain the reasons for your choice. Why do you prefer it? Write about 150-200 words.

O **Option A:** Training at the Office: You would have to come to the office every Saturday morning for eight weeks. Each training session would last from 9AM to 12PM.

O **Option B:** Training at a Training Centre: You would have to visit the training centre every Tuesday evening for 12 weeks. Each training session would last from 6:30PM to 8:30PM.

Both options have some advantages, and I can see why some employees might prefer Option B. If I had to make a choice, however, there are several reasons why I would go for Option A.

First, although I am happy that the company is providing free computer training, I would prefer to finish the training as quickly as possible. The Tuesday evening training takes four weeks longer than the Saturday morning training, so the former is not a good option for me.

Second, I learn better when I am fresh and not tired. The Tuesday training would take place in the evenings after I have already worked a full day, but the Saturday training takes place in the mornings when I would feel much less tired, which makes it a better choice for me.

Finally, I would prefer not to spend a lot of time travelling to and from the training location. The Tuesday training is 30 minutes away from the office, so I would have to spend time going there. In contrast, I live near the office, so it would be more convenient for me to train there.

So for the reasons that I have outlined, I feel Option A is the better choice.

205 words

Response to Additional Topic 2.7

| Compare your response to Additional Topic 2.7 on page 69 with the one written by a test expert below. As with every response in this book, the expert's response would probably get a score of 11 – 12.

Writing Task 2: Responding to Survey Questions	26 minutes
Read the following information. **Company Event** Your company is planning a special lunch event in July. Your manager wants to know whether you think it would be better to have a barbeque at a local beach, or to go to a popular local restaurant that sells fresh seafood.	**Choose the option that you prefer. Explain the reasons for your choice. Why do you prefer it? What problems are there with the other choice? Write about 150-200 words.** O **Option A:** Beach Barbeque: The company will supply all food and drinks. O **Option B:** Restaurant Lunch: The company will repay up to $50 per employee for food / drinks.

Both options have some advantages, and I can see why some of my co-workers might choose Option B. On the whole, however, there are several reasons why Option A would be my preference.

For one thing, I think the beach barbecue would be better value for employees. With this option, the company will pay for all of the food and drinks that people consume, so employees will not have to pay anything. At the restaurant, however, the company will only cover $50 of the cost of food and drinks. If employees want to eat or drink something expensive, their bill might be more than $50 and they would have to pay the extra cost. This would stop some people from having a good time.

For another thing, at a barbecue there are usually a wide variety of foods, including meat, vegetables and salads, and fish. This means that everyone will find something they enjoy. At a seafood restaurant, however, the options are likely to be very limited for those employees who do not like fish. I know of at least three people in my department who really dislike fish and seafood, so I think this choice would be bad for them.

So as far as I am concerned, Option A is the better choice.

214 words

Response to Additional Topic 2.8

Compare your response to Additional Topic 2.8 on page 69 with the one written by a test expert below. As with every response in this book, the expert's response would probably get a score of 11 – 12.

Writing Task 2: Responding to Survey Questions	26 minutes

ⓘ Read the following information.	**ⓘ** Choose the option that you prefer. Explain the reasons for your choice. Why do you prefer it? What problems are there with the other choice? Write about 150-200 words.
Facilities at Work	
The company where you work has a child care facility where parents can leave young children during the day. Not many people currently use the child care facility, so the company owner is thinking of replacing it with a fitness centre that would be open for all employees to use. The owner wants all workers to answer an opinion survey.	**O Option A:** Fitness Centre: The company should replace the child care facility with a fitness centre. **O Option B:** Child Care Facility: The company should keep the child care facility.

Both options have some advantages, and I can see why some people might prefer Option B. If I had to make a choice, however, there are several reasons why I would go for Option A.

For one thing, having a fitness centre in the office would make it easy for workers to exercise. Many studies have shown that those who exercise regularly are healthier, so the fitness centre might reduce the number of days when employees cannot work due to illness. This would probably benefit the company. Unlike the fitness centre, the child care facility can only be used by a small proportion of employees – those who have children – so the benefit to the company is likely to be smaller.

For another thing, although there are several gyms located near the office, most of them cost $100 per month or so. Having a fitness centre in the office would therefore help many employees save money. It would also help them save time because they would not have to travel to a separate location in order to work out. A child care facility might help some workers save time, but not money. The reason is that the government already helps citizens pay for child care expenses.

So for the reasons that I have outlined, I feel Option A is the better choice.

221 words

Response to Additional Topic 2.9

Compare your response to Additional Topic 2.9 on page 70 with the one written by a test expert below. As with every response in this book, the expert's response would probably get a score of 11 – 12.

Writing Task 2: Responding to Survey Questions	26 minutes

 Read the following information.

Working from Home

Your company is planning to allow some employees to work from home for up to three days each week. Your manager wants to know whether working from home would be suitable for you or not, and why.

 Choose the option that you prefer. Explain the reasons for your choice. Why do you prefer it? Write about 150-200 words.

O **Option A:** Work from Home: You would like to work from home up to three days each week, and you think the job you do and your home situation make working from home possible.

O **Option B:** Not Working from Home: You would prefer to continue working at the office every day. You think the work you do and your home situation would make working from home hard.

Both options have some advantages, and I can see why some employees might prefer Option B. If I had to make a choice, however, there are several reasons why I would go for Option A.

First, I live very far from the office and so working from home would save me time and help me work better. On most days, my commute takes at least one hour. By the time I get to work, I am often tired and it is hard for me to work effectively. I would be more efficient if I could work from home three days every week, because I would not be tired from commuting, so working from home would be good for me as well as beneficial for the company.

Second, my work schedule is generally flexible. On some days I meet clients in person, but on other days, I talk to them on the telephone. On days when I need to meet customers in person, I would obviously need to be in the office, but on the other days, I could easily communicate with them from home. This means that my job is very suitable for working from home for at least a few days each week.

So for the reasons that I have outlined, I feel Option A is definitely the better choice for me.

223 words

Response to Additional Topic 2.10

Compare your response to Additional Topic 2.10 on page 70 with the one written by a test expert below. As with every response in this book, the expert's response would probably get a score of 11 – 12.

Writing Task 2: Responding to Survey Questions	26 minutes

ℹ️ Read the following information.	**ℹ️ Choose the option that you prefer. Explain the reasons for your choice. Why do you prefer it? What problems are there with the other choice? Write about 150-200 words.**
City Development You live in a small city. A forested area in the northern part of the city is currently undeveloped. The city council is considering two options for this area – either cutting down the forest to build a shopping centre, or turning the forest into a recreational area where people can enjoy outdoor activities. The city council wants all residents to give their opinion.	O **Option A:** Shopping Centre: The shopping centre would have around 30 stores, plus a movie theatre, and a play area for children. O **Option B:** Recreational Area: The recreational area would have trails for hiking and biking in summer and cross-country skiing in winter.

Both options have some advantages, and I can see why some residents of the city might choose Option A. On the whole, however, there are several reasons why Option B would be my preference.

For one thing, I think a recreational area would be great for local residents. There is nothing like this in the town already, so anybody who wants to enjoy their free time outdoors must travel to other areas. In contrast, the town already has several shopping malls, so another one is unlikely to bring local people much benefit.

For another thing, I think a recreational area designed for summer and winter activities might bring tourists to the town who would spend money in local shops and restaurants. No other nearby town has a similar recreational area, but all of them have shopping centres, so the former is more likely to appeal to tourists and benefit the local economy.

Finally, these days many people are interested in protecting the environment. As far as I am concerned, turning the forested area into a place for hiking, biking, and skiing is better for the environment than cutting down the trees to build a shopping mall. I am confident that many others will share my view.

So as far as I am concerned, Option B is the better choice.

219 words

INDEX of USEFUL LANGUAGE

This list includes useful words and phrases that you can copy and use in your own responses to Task 1 or Task 2 topics. Study the words and phrases carefully to understand how to use them correctly.

— is not guaranteed	*Use these words to say that something may not happen or may be different than expected*
— is the better choice	*Use these words when you want to say which of two options is better; note that it is incorrect to say "the best choice" if you are referring to a choice between just two options*
— outweigh the advantages of ...	*Use this phrase to say that one thing has more advantages than something else; for example, you might say something like "The benefits of Option B outweigh the advantages of Option A."*
A small proportion of ...	*Use these words to refer to only a small part of something or some group; for example, you might say "A small proportion of employees would support Option A;" note that you could replace "small" with "large" or "significant"*
According to ...	*Use this phrase to introduce information that you learned from somebody or some source*
Again, ...	*Use this word to repeat a point that you have already made earlier; note that it is often natural to refer back to a point you have already made, but be careful about repeating points using exactly the same words, which may reduce your overall score*
Alternatively, ...	*Use this word to introduce an alternative idea or suggestion*
An average of ...	*Use these words to give the average number of something; for example, you might write "The average number of people who came to each class was just seven."*
And second, ...	*Use this phrase to introduce a second point, opinion, problem, and so on; note that including "And" suggests that this is your final point*
Annually	*Use this word as an alternative to words "yearly" or "each year"*
As a result, ...	*Use this phrase to explain or introduce something that will happen because of something or somebody else*
As far as I am concerned, ...	*Use this phrase to introduce your opinion about something; note that this phrase sounds especially natural if other people might hold an alternative opinion*

As far as I know, …	*Use this phrase to indicate your knowledge about something; note that the phrase suggests you are not certain your knowledge is right*
As well	*Use this phrase as an alternative to "too"; note that "as well" almost always comes at the end of the sentence*
As you know, …	*Use this phrase to introduce some information that the person reading your email already knows*
As you requested, …	*Use this phrase to introduce some information that somebody has asked you to give*
At first …	*Use these words to say what happened or how something was at the beginning; contrast these words with a phrase like "but soon …" or "after a while …"*
At the moment …	*Use this phrase to talk about something that is currently true or happening now*
Both options have some advantages, …	*Use these words to make it clear that you believe two choices both have benefits*
By far	*Use this phrase when you are comparing two things to say that one option is much better than the other option*
Discuss (something) further	*Use these words to talk about discussing something in more detail*
Especially …	*Use this word to emphasize something; for example, "Many people would be especially happy to have a new fitness centre."*
Everyone else	*Use these words to compare the situation for one or more groups of people with the situation for another group people*
Finally, …	*Use this phrase to introduce a final point or reason for your view*
First, …	*Use this word to introduce a first point, opinion, problem, and so on*
Firstly, …	*Use this word to give your first reason or point about something*
For another thing, …	*Use this phrase to introduce a second point or reason for your view*
For example, …	*Use this phrase to introduce an example that supports your opinion or reason about something*
For instance, …	*Use this phrase as an alternative to "For example, …" when you want to introduce an example that supports your view about a topic*
For one thing, …	*Use this phrase to introduce one point or reason for your opinion*
For the reasons that I have outlined, …	*Use this phrase to refer back to reasons you have explained earlier in your response*

For these two reasons, ...	*Use this phrase before you summarize your opinion about a topic or the option you chose*
Give me a call so ...	*Use these words to ask the other person to get in touch with you for a particular reason*
Have you considered ... ?	*Use this phrase to suggest something that you and other people could do; note that the sentence should end with a question mark; also note that after "considered" you should use the –ing form of a word*
How about ... ?	*Use this phrase to suggest something that you and other people could do; note that the word after "about" should be an –ing word like "going" or "doing"; also note that the sentence should end with a question mark*
However, ...	*Use this word to introduce some contrasting information*
I am confident that ...	*Use this phrase to express an opinion you are confident is true*
I am hoping that ...	*Use this phrase as a less formal alternative to "It is my hope that ..."*
I am sad to say that ...	*Use these words to introduce some negative information; note that you could replace the word "sad" with "sorry"*
I am sure that ...	*Use this phrase to express an opinion you are certain about*
I am sure that other people ...	*Use this phrase when you want to introduce an opinion that other people are likely to share*
I am worried that ...	*Use these words to introduce something you are worried about; note that you can use "concerned" instead of "worried"*
I am writing to complain about ...	*Use this phrase to introduce something you wish to complain about*
I am writing to tell you about ...	*Use this phrase to explain your reason for writing to somebody*
I can honestly say that ...	*Use these words when you wish to express a strong, honest opinion about something*
I can see why some ...	*Use these words to introduce an opinion that some people might hold about something*
I have heard that ...	*Use this phrase to introduce some information that you heard from somebody else, read in a newspaper, and so on*
I have heard that ...	*Use these words to introduce information that you learned from somebody or some source*
I hope to hear from you soon	*Use this expression to close an email in which you have asked somebody to contact you*

I hope you …	*Use this phrase to express a thing you hope about somebody else*
I know of …	*Use this phrase to introduce your knowledge of something; note that this phrase suggests your knowledge may be something you have experienced yourself or something you were told about*
I look forward to a positive response	*Use this phrase to close an email in which you have asked somebody to do something for you*
I look forward to hearing from you	*Use this phrase to close an email if you have asked the other person to contact you or give you some information*
I see two problems with …	*Use these words to introduce problems or issues with something, such as somebody's plan*
I was told that …	*Use these words to say what somebody told you*
I will definitely …	*Use these words to introduce something that you are certain you will do in the future*
I would like to thank you …	*Use these words to introduce something that you would like to say thank you to other people for*
I would like you to …	*Use this phrase when you want another person to perform a particular task or take a specific action*
I would prefer to …	*Use these words to express a preference about something*
If I had to make a choice, …	*Use this phrase to express a choice about a hypothetical situation*
In a few years …	*Use these words to say what will (or might) happen in several years*
In addition, …	*Use this phrase to introduce a second or third point*
In consequence, …	*Use this phrase to introduce a result of something.*
In contrast, …	*Use this phrase when you want to introduce an idea or opinion that contrasts with something you have already mentioned*
In fact, …	*Use this phrase to emphasize a point you would like to make or to compare what some people think with what is actually true*
In my opinion, …	*Use this phrase to introduce your opinion about something*
In my view …	*Use this phrase as an alternative to "in my opinion"*
In other words, …	*Use this phrase to clarify the meaning of something you have just mentioned or explained*
In particular, …	*Use these words to introduce a point you wish to emphasize*

In terms of …	*Use this phrase to introduce a topic; for example, write "In terms of the best place to go, …" and then discuss a good place to go.*
In the long term	*Use this phrase to talk about something that will happen a fairly long time from now or that will take a long time to show an effect*
In the neighborhood	*Use this phrase either to mean something that is close to where you live; for example, "There are many nice shops in my neighborhood" or "There are several cafés in the neighborhood of the office."*
Inexpensive	*Use this word as a relatively formal alternative to "cheap"*
It is my hope that …	*Use these words as a somewhat formal alternative to "I hope that"*
Let me know (if) …	*Use these words to say somebody can contact you about something*
Many …	*Use this word to mean "many people" in a phrase like "many believe" or "many think"; note that you can use other words in the same way, such as "some think" or "others feel" or "most believe"*
Many studies have shown that …	*Use these words to introduce research or evidence to support your opinion about something*
Moreover, …	*Use this word to introduce an opinion or point about something after you have already introduced a previous opinion or point*
My feeling is that …	*Use this phrase to express your opinion or feeling about something*
No earlier than …	*Use this phrase to talk about the earliest time or date when something will happen*
No later than …	*Use this phrase to talk about the latest time or date when something will happen*
Not only … , but also …	*Use this paired phrase to introduce two related ideas; for example, "Option A not only benefits customers, but also helps employees."*
Not only that, but …	*Use this phrase to introduce a second point you would like to make; note that you cannot use this phrase to introduce your first point*
Of course, …	*Use this phrase when you want to say something that most people would consider to be obvious*
On the one hand, …	*Use this phrase to introduce one idea that will be contrast with another idea that you later introduce with "On the other hand".*
On the other hand, …	*Use this phrase to introduce a second idea that contrasts with an earlier idea you introduced with "On the one hand".*
On the whole, …	*Use this phrase to introduce your opinion about something; note that this phrase suggests you think another view has some benefits*

One major benefit of …	*Use these words to introduce an important benefit of something; note that you can replace "One major benefit" with other phrases like "Another benefit" or "An additional benefit"*
Or so	*Use these words as an alternative to "approximately"; note that "or so" should come after the number (e.g., "$50 or so"), not before it.*
Or something like that	*Use these words to make it clear that you cannot remember something exactly, or did not see something clearly; for example, you might say the cost was "$50 or something like that."*
Particularly …	*Use this word to emphasize something; for example, "A new fitness centre would not be particularly useful for residents in the building."*
Please contact me / Give me a call if you have any questions …	*Use either of these phrases to let the person reading your email know that he or she can get in touch with you for more details.*
Please could you …	*Use these words to request that somebody do something for you*
Please find a way to …	*Use these words to ask somebody to do something for you, especially something that might be difficult*
Secondly, …	*Use this word to give your second reason or point about something*
Since last month, …	*Use these words to talk about something that started last month and is still true; note that after this phrase, it would be natural to use present perfect tense (e.g., "have done" or "have been doing")*
So	*Use this word to introduce a conclusion about something or to summarize your opinion when you begin your concluding paragraph*
Sort (the problem) out	*Use this phrasal verb to describe solving or fixing a problem; note that "sort … out" and "sort out …" are both correct English; also note that you can "sort out an issue" or "a situation" and so on.*
Still others	*Use these words to say what a third group of people might do; note that these words only sound natural when used in a list something like "Some people … Other people .. Still others …"*
Strongly advise …	*Use these words to give a strong recommendation to somebody*
Such as …	*Use these words to give an example of something; note that "such as" typically comes in the middle of a sentence, and in most cases it is not natural to begin a sentence with these words*
Supposed to be …	*Use these words to say what should have happened or should have been true but did not actually happen or was not actually true*
Tend to	*Use this phrase to describe something that often happens or is usually true; for instance, you might say something like "people who live in cities tend to go out more often than people …"*

Thank you in advance	*Use this phrase to close an email in which you have asked somebody to do something for you, especially something that might take time or cost money*
The former	*Use this phrase to refer back to the first of two things you have already mentioned*
The latter	*Use this phrase to refer back to the second of two things you have already mentioned*
The main reason is that ...	*Use these words to introduce the most important reason why you (or somebody) holds an opinion or why something happened; note that you can replace "The main reason" with other phrases like "Another reason" or "A second reason"*
The other day	*Use these words to mean something like "a few days ago"*
The reason is that ...	*Use this phrase to introduce the reason for something*
The vast majority of ...	*Use this phrase to talk about something that is mostly true or that many people believe; for example, you might say "The vast majority of people would support Option A, in my view."*
There are several reasons why ...	*Use this phrase to introduce several reasons for something*
Therefore, ...	*Use this word to introduce a conclusion about something*
These days, ...	*Use this phrase to introduce a situation that is currently true*
This caused ...	*Use these words to say what happened as a result of something*
This means that ...	*Use these words either to clarify the meaning of an idea you have just mentioned, or to talk about the result of something*
To give an example, ...	*Use this phrase as an alternative to "For example, ..." or "For instance, ..."*
To Whom It May Concern	*Use this phrase to begin a formal email when you don't know the name of the person you are writing to*
Unfortunately ...	*Use this word to introduce something you have a negative opinion about, or to describe a negative event that happened*
Why don't we ... ?	*Use this phrase to suggest something that you and other people could do; note that the sentence should end with a question mark*
Would you be willing to ... ?	*Use these words to ask somebody if he or she would do something; note that the sentence should end with a question mark*

Made in the USA
Lexington, KY
15 September 2017

HORSE LOVER'S

SCROLL SAW PATTERNS

PATTERNS FOR:
- ✔ CLOCKS
- ✔ SHELVES
- ✔ PLAQUES
- ✔ GIFTS
- ...AND MORE!

Scroll Saw
FAVORITES

BY JOHN A. NELSON